STUDENT UNIT GUIDE

GW00720592

AS Sport & Physical Education
UNIT 1
AQA

Module 1: Physiological and Psychological Factors which Improve Performance

Sue Young and Symond Burrows

Philip Allan Updates
Market Place
Deddington
Oxfordshire
OX15 0SE

tel: 01869 338652
fax: 01869 337590
e-mail: sales@philipallan.co.uk
www.philipallan.co.uk

ISBN-13: 978-1-84489-024-8
ISBN-10: 1-84489-024-4

This Guide has been written specifically to support students preparing for the
AQA AS Sport and Physical Education Unit 2 examination. The content has been
neither approved nor endorsed by AQA and remains the sole responsibility of
the authors.

Printed by MPG Books, Bodmin

Environmental information
The paper on which this title is printed is sourced from managed, sustainable
forests.

Contents

Introduction

■ ■ ■

Content Guidance

■ ■ ■

Questions and Answers

Introduction

About this guide

This unit guide is written to help you prepare for Unit 1 which examines the content of the **Module 1: Physiological and Psychological Factors which Improve Performance**. There are three sections to this guide:

- **Introduction** — this provides advice on how to use the unit guide, an explanation of the skills required by Unit 1 and suggestions for effective revision.
- **Content Guidance** — this summarises the specification content of Module 1.
- **Questions and Answers** — this provides examples of questions from various topic areas, together with student answers and examiner's comments on how these could have been improved.

An effective way to use this guide is to read through this introduction at the beginning of your course to familiarise yourself with the skills required for AS Physical Education. Try to make a habit of following the study skills and revision advice offered in this section. It may also help to refer back to this information at regular intervals during your course.

The Content Guidance section will be useful when revising a particular topic because it highlights the key points. You may want to tick off topic areas as you learn them to make sure that you have revised everything thoroughly.

The Questions and Answers section will provide useful practice when preparing for the unit test. This practice should increase your awareness of exam-technique issues and maximise your chances of success.

The specification

Module 1 requires you to show understanding of how performance is influenced by physical and mental wellbeing and preparation. It is important to be able to link and interrelate physiological and psychological factors, and to explain how they affect sports preparation and performance.

In order to make a good start to Module 1, it is important to have a close look at the specification. If you do not have a copy of this, either ask your teacher for one or download it from the AQA website, **www.aqa.org.uk**.

In addition to describing the content of the module (which sometimes provides detail that could earn you marks), the specification gives information about the unit tests. It is important for you to understand the following key terms used:

- **analysis** — a detailed examination to find the meaning or essential features of a topic

- **characteristic** — a feature or key distinguishing quality
- **definition** — a clear, concise statement of the meaning of a term
- **understanding** — showing clear knowledge of topics covered

The specification also provides information about other skills required in Module 1. For example, using the experience gained by performing practical activities as a basis for improving physiological and psychological understanding. You also need to develop the skills of interpreting and drawing graphs and diagrams.

Finally, in addition to looking at the specification, it would be useful for you to read the examiners' reports and mark schemes from previous Unit 1 tests (these are available from AQA). These documents show you the depth of knowledge that examiners are looking for, as well as pointing out common mistakes and providing advice on how to achieve good grades.

Study skills and revision strategies

All students need good study skills to be successful. This section provides advice and guidance on how to study AS Sport & Physical Education, together with some strategies for effective revision.

Organising your notes

PE students often accumulate a large quantity of notes, so it is useful to keep this information in an organised manner. The presentation is important; good notes should always be clear and concise. You could try organising your notes under main headings and subheadings, with key points highlighted using capitals, italics or colour. Numbered lists can be useful, as can the presentation of information in table form and simple diagrams. For example:

Organising your time

It is a good idea to make a revision timetable to ensure you use your time effectively. This should allow enough time to cover *all* the relevant material. However, it must also be realistic. For many students, revising for longer than an hour at a time becomes counterproductive, so allow time for short relaxation breaks or exercise to refresh the body and mind.

Improving your memory

There are several ways to improve the effectiveness of your memory. Organising the material will help, especially if you use topic headings, numbered lists and diagrams. Reviewing and condensing your notes will also be useful, as will discussing topics with teachers and other students. Using mnemonics (memory aids) can make a big difference. For example, a mnemonic for the key characteristics of skill is:

- **F**luent
- **L**earned
- **A**esthetic
- **G**oal-directed

Revision strategies

To revise a topic effectively, you should work carefully through your notes, using a copy of the specification to make sure everything is covered. Summarise your notes on the key points using the tips offered above. Topic cue cards, with a summary of key facts and visual representations of the material, can be useful. These are easily carried around for quick revision. Finally, use the Content Guidance and Question and Answer sections in this book, discussing any problems or difficulties you have with your teachers or other students.

In many ways, you should prepare for a unit test like an athlete prepares for a major event, such as the Olympic games. An athlete trains every day for weeks or months before the event, practising the required skills in order to achieve the best result on the day. So it is with exam preparation: everything you do should contribute to your chances of success in the unit test.

The following points summarise some of the strategies that you may wish to use to make sure your revision is as effective as possible:

- Use a revision timetable.
- Ideally, spend time revising in a quiet room, sitting upright at a desk or table, with no distractions.
- Test yourself regularly to assess the effectiveness of your revision. Ask yourself: 'Which techniques work best?' 'What are the gaps in my knowledge?' Remember to revise what you *don't* know.
- Practise past paper questions to highlight gaps in your knowledge and understanding and to improve your technique. You will also become more familiar with the terminology used in exam questions.
- Spend time doing 'active revision', such as:
  - discussing topics with fellow students or teachers
  - summarising your notes
  - compiling revision cue cards
  - answering previous test questions and self-checking against mark schemes

Preparation for exams is a very personal thing — you should do what works best for you. You could also draw up, and use, a 'revision progress' table, as shown below.

Revision progress

Complete column 2 to show how far you have progressed with your revision:
- N = not revised yet
- P = partly revised
- F = fully revised

Complete column 3 to show how confident you are with the topic:
- 5 = high degree of confidence
- 1 = minimal confidence — the practice questions were poorly answered

The tables should be updated as your revision progresses.

Physiological factors

Movement

Topic	Revised (N/P/F)	Self-evaluation (1–5)
Axes and planes of the body		
Muscles and bones involved in: • sprinting/running • arm/shoulder action in overarm throwing • arm/shoulder action in racquet strokes • leg action in squats • arm action in push-ups • leg action in kicking and jumping		
Types of muscle contraction		
Antagonistic muscle action		
Classification of levers and their relationship to effective performance (mechanical disadvantage and range and speed of movement)		

Fitness

Topic	Revised (N/P/F)	Self-evaluation (1–5)
Problems with defining health and fitness		
Fitness components, definition and method of testing: • cardiorespiratory endurance • muscular endurance • strength • speed • power • flexibility • agility • balance • body composition		
Reliability and validity of fitness testing		

Respiration

Topic	Revised (N/P/F)	Self-evaluation (1–5)
Gaseous exchange in the alveoli		
Principles of diffusion		
Partial pressures		
Differences in inspired and expired air		
Differences in oxygen and carbon dioxide content of alveolar air and pulmonary blood		
Lung volumes and capacities, definitions and interpretations from a spirometer trace		
Transportation of oxygen		
The roles of haemoglobin and myoglobin		
The importance of plasma carbon dioxide in the control of breathing rate (neural control)		
Gaseous exchange at the tissues		
The effects of exercise on the dissociation of haemoglobin at the tissues		
Arteriovenous difference in oxygen and carbon dioxide		

The cardiovascular system

Topic	Revised (N/P/F)	Self-evaluation (1–5)
The cardiac cycle and action of the heart valves		
The conduction system		
Stroke volume, heart rate and cardiac output		
Nervous and hormonal influences on heart rate		
Pulmonary and systemic circulation		
Types of blood vessels; their features and functions		
The pulse		
Blood pressure		
Blood velocity		
Re-distribution of blood		
Mechanisms of venous return		
Effects of training on lung volumes, capacities and gaseous exchange in the alveoli		
Effects of training on the heart (bradycardia, athletes heart)		

Psychological factors

Defining, developing and classifying skills

Topic	Revised (N/P/F)	Self-evaluation (1–5)
The characteristics of skilled performance		
Different types of skill		
Analysing movement skills		
The application of 'classification' in the organisation and determination of practices		
Definition and characteristics of abilities		

Information processing during performance

Topic	Revised (N/P/F)	Self-evaluation (1–5)
Basic models of information processing		
Memory process		
Reaction time		
Feedback		

You need to be able to relate the information-processing requirements of movement skills to your own practical activity experiences.

Control of motor skills

Topic	Revised (N/P/F)	Self-evaluation (1–5)
Motor programmes		
Motor control		
Open-loop and closed-loop theories (Adams)		
Schema theory		
Relationship between learning and performance		
Interpretation of learning and performance curves		
The learning plateau		
Mosston's teaching styles		

Learning skills

Topic	Revised (N/P/F)	Self-evaluation (1–5)
Connectionist or association themes		
Cognitive learning theory		
Observational learning		
Phases of learning movement skills		
Methods of guidance		
Transfer of learning		
Motivation and arousal		
Practice conditions (e.g. massed versus distributed)		

It is important to revise every topic, because any area of the specification could appear in the unit test.

The unit test

Unit Test 1 consists of five questions, of which you have to answer four. Each question is worth 18 marks and the test lasts 90 minutes. The questions will assess your understanding of a mix of physiological and psychological factors that affect performance, and are subdivided into short sections.

You might be required to sketch or interpret graphs and diagrams. You have to be able to show your understanding of the specification content by using appropriate technical language in your answers.

There are a number of terms commonly used in unit tests. It is important that you understand the meaning of each of these terms and that you answer the question appropriately.
- **Compare** — point out similarities and differences.
- **Define** — give a statement, outlining what is meant by a particular term.
- **Describe** — provide an accurate account of the main points in relation to the task set.
- **Discuss** — describe and evaluate, putting forward the various opinions on a topic.
- **Explain** — give reasons to justify statements and opinions given in your answer.
- **Identify** — show understanding of unique or key characteristics.
- **State/give/list/name** — give a concise, factual answer.
- **What?/why?/where?/who?/how?** — these indicate direct questions, requiring concise answers.

Whatever the question style, you must read the wording very carefully, underline or highlight key words or phrases, think about your response and allocate time according to the number of marks available. Further advice and guidance on answering Unit 1 questions is provided in the Question and Answer section of this book.

The day of the unit test

On the day of the test, make sure that you have:
- two or more blue/black pens
- a pencil, rubber and ruler
- a watch to check the time
- water in a clear bottle to keep you hydrated
- a calculator

Make sure that you allow plenty of time to arrive, so that you are relaxed.

Read each question very carefully so that your answers are appropriate and relevant. Make sure that your writing is legible (you will not be awarded marks if the examiner cannot read what you have written). If you need more room for your answer, look for space at the bottom of the page or use the spare sheets at the end of the booklet. If you do this, alert the examiner by adding 'continued below', or 'continued on page X'.

Time is sometimes a problem. Make sure you know how long you have for the whole test. If you finish early, check your answers, adding more points to ensure you gain as many marks as possible. This is your one chance to impress the examiner — so take it!

Content
Guidance

The physiological section of Module 1 helps create a greater understanding of the structure and mechanics of the human body, the function and control of body systems and how they interlink with the physiological make-up of an individual to determine both the standard and effectiveness of performance in a wide range of physical activities.

There are four main topic areas:
- Movement
- Fitness
- Respiration
- The cardiovascular system

The psychological section of Module 1 requires you to develop and show your understanding of effective ways of acquiring and improving movement skills in a variety of physical activities. It requires you to develop theoretical understanding of skill acquisition and to use practical examples to illustrate this understanding.

There are four main topic areas:
- Defining, developing and classifying skills
- Information processing during performance
- Control of motor skills
- Learning skills

You may already be familiar with some of the information in these topic areas. However, it is important that you know and understand this information exactly as described in the specification. This summary of the specification content highlights key points. Therefore, you should find it useful when revising for the Unit 1 test.

Movement

How the body moves

Axes and planes of the body

To help explain movement, it is possible to imagine the body as having a series of imaginary sections running through it. These are called **planes of movement** and divide the body in three ways:

- The **sagittal plane** is a vertical plane that divides the body into right and left sides.
- The **frontal (coronal) plane** is a vertical plane that divides the body into front and back parts.
- The **transverse (horizontal) plane** divides the body into upper and lower parts.

When performing an activity, the body (or body parts) moves in one, two or all three, of these planes depending on the action being performed. In a full twisting somersault, for example, the gymnast moves in all three planes.

There are three **axes of movement**:

- The frontal axis runs from side to side across the body.
- The saggital axis runs from front to back.
- The vertical axis runs from top to bottom.

Most movements occurring at joints are related to both axes and planes. Flexion and extension, for example, occur in a sagittal plane about a frontal axis, whereas rotation occurs in a horizontal plane about a vertical axis

Joints, muscles and movement

These are summarised in the tables below. An agonist is a muscle that shortens under tension to produce movement.

Hinge joints

Hinge joint	Articulating bones	Movement	Agonist
Elbow	Radius, ulna and humerus	Flexion	Biceps brachii
Knee	Tibia, femur and patella	Extension	Triceps brachii
Ankle	Tibia, fibula and talus	Flexion	Hamstrings
		Extension	Quadriceps
		Plantarflexion	Gastrocnemius
		Dorsiflexion	Tibialis anterior

Ball-and-socket joints

Joint	Articulating bones	Movement	Agonist
Hip	Acetabulum of the pelvis and femur	Flexion	Ilio psoas
		Extension	Gluteus maximus
		Outward rotation	Gluteus maximus
		Inward rotation	Gluteus minimus
		Abduction	Gluteus medius
		Adduction	Adductors (longus, brevis and magnus)
Shoulder	Glenoid fossa of the scapula and humerus	Flexion	Anterior deltoid
		Extension	Latissimus dorsi
		Outward rotation	Infraspinatus
		Inward rotation	Subscapularis
		Abduction	Middle deltoid
		Adduction	Pectoralis major

Gliding joints

Joint	Articulating bones	Movement	Agonist
Spine	Vertebral arches	Flexion	Rectus abdominus
		Extension	Sacrospinalis
		Lateral flexion	External obliques
		Rotation (to the opposite side)	External obliques
Shoulder girdle	Clavicle and scapula	Elevation	Trapezius part 1
		Depression	Trapezius part 4
		Upward rotation	Trapezius part 2
		Downward rotation	Rhomboids
		Abduction	Serratus anterior
		Adduction	Trapezius part 3

Practical examples

You are expected to know the muscles and bones involved in the following common movements:

- leg action in sprinting and running
- arm and shoulder action in overarm throwing and racquet strokes
- leg action in squats
- arm action in push-ups
- leg action in kicking and jumping

Right leg action in kicking
- Hip joint — flexion
- Agonist — ilio psoas
- Antagonist — gluteus maximus
- Knee joint — extension
- Antagonist — quadriceps (rectus femoris)
- Agonist — hamstrings (bicep femoris)

Leg action in squats (downward phase)
- Hip joint — flexion
- Agonist — ilio psoas
- Antagonist — gluteus maximus
- Knee joint — flexion
- Agonist — hamstrings (bicep femoris)
- Antagonist — quadriceps (rectus femoris)

(Reverse movements for upward phase)

Right shoulder and arm actions during the beginning of the tennis serve
- Shoulder — abduction
- Agonist — deltoid (middle)
- Antagonist — latissimus dorsi
- Elbow joint — flexion
- Agonist — biceps brachii
- Antagonist — triceps brachii

Joints and levers

A lever has three main components:
- a pivot (fulcrum)
- the weight to be moved (resistance)
- a source of energy (effort or force)

In the body, the skeleton forms a system of levers that allows us to move. The bones act as the levers, the joints are the fulcrums and the effort is provided by the muscle.

The main functions of a lever are:
- to increase the speed at which the body can move
- to increase the resistance that a given effort can move

Classification of levers
There are three types of lever:
- **First-order lever** — the fulcrum is between the effort and the resistance. First-order levers can increase both the effects of the effort and the speed of the body.

An example can be seen in the movement of the head and neck during flexion and extension.

- **Second-order lever** — the resistance lies between the fulcrum and the effort. Second-order levers are generally thought to increase only the effect of the effort or force. Plantarflexion of the ankle involves the use of a second-order lever.
- **Third-order lever** — the effort lies between the fulcrum and the resistance. Third-order levers are responsible for most movements of the human body. They can increase the ability of the body to move quickly, but in terms of applying force they are very inefficient. An example can be seen in the forearm during flexion of the elbow.

The type of lever at each joint and the surrounding muscles affect the movement, as does the angle of pull and the length of the lever.

Angle of pull

The angle of pull is crucial for the efficiency of the pulling force of a muscle. It is calculated by measuring the angle between the insertion of the muscle and the position of the joint. When your arms are by your side the angle of pull is small. As flexion of the elbow occurs, the angle increases. When the angle of pull is around 90° the muscle works more effectively.

Length of lever

The longer the resistance arm of the lever, the greater the speed at the end of it. This means that if the arm is fully extended when bowling or passing, the ball will travel with most force and at the greatest speed. The use of a cricket bat, racquet or golf club effectively extends the arm and allows more force to be exerted.

Muscles and effective movement

Types of muscular contraction

A muscle can contract in three different ways, depending on the muscle action that is required.

Concentric contraction

The muscle shortens under tension. For example, during the upward phase of an arm curl, the biceps brachii performs a concentric contraction as it shortens to produce flexion of the elbow.

Eccentric contraction

The muscle lengthens under tension (and does not relax). When a muscle contracts eccentrically it is acting as a brake to help control the movement of the body part during negative work — for example, landing from a standing jump. Here, the quadriceps muscles are performing negative work as they are supporting the weight of the body during landing. The knee joint is in the flexed position but the quadriceps muscles are unable to relax as the weight of the body ensures that they lengthen under tension.

Isometric contraction

The muscle contracts without lengthening or shortening. The result is that no movement occurs. An isometric contraction occurs when a muscle acts as a fixator or against a resistance.

Muscle function

A muscle can perform three functions:

- **agonist** — the muscle shortens under tension to produce movement
- **antagonist** — the muscle relaxes or lengthens to allow the agonist to shorten
- **fixator** — the muscle increases in tension, but no movement occurs. A fixator is normally located at the joint where the origin of the agonist occurs. For example, in the upward phase of an arm curl, the bicep brachii contracts and is the agonist. Its origin is in the shoulder, so the deltoid acts as a fixator during this movement.

Antagonistic muscle action

Using flexion of the elbow as an example, the biceps brachii contracts, and is responsible for the movement. It is said to be acting as an agonist or prime mover. An antagonistic muscle is one that works in opposition to the agonist. When the biceps brachii is contracting, the triceps brachii is lengthening and acting as the antagonist. When one muscle is acting as an agonist and the other is acting as the antagonist, the muscles are said to be working together as a pair to produce the required movement. This is called **antagonistic muscle action**.

If we look at flexion of the knee, the hamstrings are the agonists and the quadriceps are the antagonists.

There can be more than one agonist acting at a joint, although this does depend on the type of movement.

What the examiner will expect you to be able to do

- You are required to know how the body moves in relation to planes and axes, during specific exercises.
- You might be asked to classify a lever as first, second or third order and to relate the lever to effective performance.
- Make sure that you learn the joint, muscle and movement tables, the types of muscle contraction and muscle function. You might be asked to apply this knowledge.

Fitness

Definitions of fitness and health

Fitness can be difficult to define because it means different things to different people. Some people may think they are fit if they can run for the bus or play football in the park without getting out of breath, whereas active people may look at resting heart rate or heart rate recovery after exercise as an indication of fitness. One generic definition of fitness is **the ability to perform daily tasks without undue fatigue**.

It is important to remember that these daily tasks will be quite different for an elite performer compared with a non-athletic person. The fitness requirements of physical activities also vary. For example, the 100 m sprint requires the body to work anaerobically with great strength, speed and power, whereas the marathon requires good muscular endurance and good aerobic capacity.

Health is often defined as **being free from mental and physical disease**.

Components of fitness

- **Physical or health components** include aerobic capacity, strength, flexibility and body composition.
- **Skill or motor components** include speed, balance, reaction time, coordination, agility and power.

Definitions of components of fitness, together with methods of testing, are given in the table below.

Component	Definition	Method of testing
Cardiorespiratory endurance (stamina, VO_2(max), aerobic fitness)	The ability to take in and use oxygen during prolonged exercise in order to delay the onset of fatigue	Douglas bag Multi-stage fitness test Step test
Strength — maximum	The maximum force a muscle can exert in a single voluntary contraction	Hand-grip dynamometer
Strength — elastic	Ability to overcome resistance with a high-speed contraction	Wingate test
Strength — endurance	Ability of a muscle to perform repeated contractions and to withstand fatigue	NCF abdominal curl
Flexibility — static	Range of movement round a joint	Sit-and-reach test
Flexibility — dynamic	Resistance of a joint to movement	Shoulder flexibility test

Component	Definition	Method of testing
Body composition	Physiological make-up of an individual in terms of the distribution of fat and lean body mass	Skin-fold test
Speed	How fast a person can cover a specified distance or how quickly a body part can be put into motion	30 m sprint
*Balance	Ability to keep the centre of mass over the base of support	Balance board
Agility	Ability to move and position the body quickly and effectively while under control	Illinois agility run
Power	The amount of work performed per unit of time; the product of strength and speed	Vertical jump

*Balance can be static (e.g. a handstand) or dynamic (retained in motion)

Validity and reliability of testing

When carrying out the various fitness tests, it is important to consider their validity and reliability.

Validity — does the test measure exactly what it sets out to? For example, the 'sit-and-reach' test for flexibility only covers the hamstrings and lower back. Therefore, it is a valid test for the lower body but not for the upper body.

Is the test sport specific? It is important to conduct a test that replicates sporting actions and uses the muscles in the same way they are used in the performer's activity. For example, the 'multi-stage fitness' test involves running, so it is valid for a games player where a lot of running is involved but less so for a cyclist or a swimmer.

Reliability — is the test accurate? In order for the 'step test' to be reliable, it is impor-tant to ensure that the procedure is correctly maintained, i.e. everyone who completes the test should do so at the same rate, height and cadence and there should be full extension between steps.

Factors to take into account when testing include the following:
- The tester should be experienced.
- The equipment should be standardised.
- Sequencing of tests is important.
- The performers should be motivated to complete the test to the best of their abilities.
- Tests should be repeated to minimise the effects of human error.

What the examiner will expect you to be able to do

You will be expected to understand the difference between validity and reliability and to be able to apply these concepts to the various fitness tests.

Respiration
The mechanics of breathing

Air moves from an area of high pressure to an area of low pressure. The greater the difference in pressure, the faster air will flow. Changing the volume of the thoracic cavity alters the pressure of air in the lungs. Increasing the volume decreases the pressure, drawing air into the lungs from outside. Reducing the volume increases the pressure and air is forced out of the lungs.

- Inspiration — the volume of the thoracic cavity increases because of muscular contraction
- Expiration — the volume of the thoracic cavity is reduced

Respiratory muscles

Ventilation phase	Muscles used during breathing at rest	Muscles used during exercise
Inspiration	Diaphragm External intercostals	Diaphragm External intercostals Sternocleidomastoid Pectoralis minor
Expiration	Diaphragm and external intercostals relax (passive process)	Internal intercostals Abdominals

Note that during exercise, additional muscles are used during inspiration and that expiration is active, rather than passive.

Gaseous exchange

Gaseous exchange in the lungs

Gaseous exchange involves the **diffusion** of a gas from an area of high concentration to an area of low concentration down a concentration gradient until an equilibrium is reached. In the lungs, the vast network of alveoli and the surrounding blood capillaries create a large surface area and this helps diffusion to occur. The thin alveolar and capillary walls also reduce the diffusion distance between the air in the alveoli and the blood. The rate of diffusion of an average person is approximately 250 cm³ of oxygen per minute at rest but this can rise to over 5 dm³ of oxygen per minute during exercise.

The idea of **partial pressure** is often used when describing gaseous exchange. All gases exert a pressure. Oxygen makes up approximately 21% of air, so it exerts a partial pressure. Gases flow from an area of high pressure to an area of low pressure. As oxygen moves from the alveoli to the blood and then to the muscle, its partial pressure in each has to be successively lower.

The exchange of gases in the lungs takes place between alveolar air and blood flowing through the lung (pulmonary) capillaries. Oxygen enters the blood from the alveoli because the partial pressure of oxygen in the alveoli (100 mmHg) is higher than the partial pressure of oxygen in the incoming blood vessels (40 mmHg). This is because oxygen has been removed by the working muscles. Therefore, the concentration of oxygen in the blood is lower and so is its partial pressure. The difference between any two pressures is referred to as the pressure gradient and the bigger this gradient the faster diffusion will be. Oxygen diffuses from the alveoli into the blood until the pressure is equal in both.

The movement of carbon dioxide occurs similarly, but from the blood to the alveoli, because the partial pressure of carbon dioxide in the alveoli (40 mmHg) is lower than that of carbon dioxide in the blood (45 mmHg).

Differences between inspired and expired air

Inspired air contains more oxygen than expired air; expired air contains more carbon dioxide than inspired air. The percentage concentrations of gases in inspired and expired air are shown in the table below.

	Inspired air at rest	Expired air at rest	Expired air during exercise
Oxygen	21.0%	16.4%	14.0%
Carbon dioxide	0.04%	4.0%	6.0%

Gaseous exchange at the tissues

This takes place between arterial blood, flowing through the tissue capillaries, and the cells. Oxygen diffuses out of the arterial blood and into the cells because the partial pressure of oxygen is higher (100 mmHg) in the blood than in the cells (40 mmHg).

Arterio-venous difference

This is the difference between the oxygen content of the arterial blood arriving at the muscles and the venous blood leaving the muscles. At rest, the arterio-venous difference is low because not much oxygen is required by the muscles. However, during exercise much more oxygen is needed, so the arterio-venous difference is high.

content guidance

This increase affects gaseous exchange in the alveoli. There is a higher concentration of carbon dioxide, and a lower level of oxygen in the venous blood returning to the heart (and then being sent to the lungs). This increases the diffusion gradients of both gases.

Training also increases the arterio-venous difference because trained performers can extract more oxygen from the blood.

Gaseous exchange overview

The following diagram highlights the differences in the partial pressures of oxygen and carbon dioxide in the alveoli, blood and muscle tissue and also shows the arterio-venous difference.

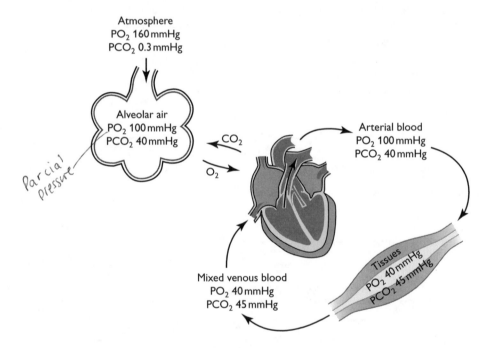

Transport of oxygen

Only about 3% of oxygen dissolves in plasma; 97% combines with **haemoglobin** to form **oxyhaemoglobin**. When fully saturated, each haemoglobin molecule carries four oxygen molecules. At the tissues, oxygen dissociates from haemoglobin because of the lower partial pressure of oxygen in the tissues. In the muscle cells, oxygen is taken up by **myoglobin**.

Myoglobin occurs in the sarcoplasm of muscle cells. It has a high affinity for oxygen, which means that it can act as an oxygen store. During exercise, there is increased cellular respiration. As a result, the partial pressure of oxygen in the cells drops to the point where myoglobin gives up its oxygen to the mitochondria.

Haemoglobin saturation

The relationship between oxygen and haemoglobin can be represented by the oxyhaemoglobin dissociation curve:

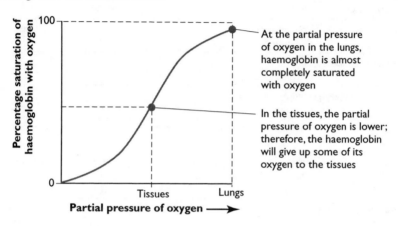

During exercise, there is an increased demand for oxygen. Exercise creates conditions that cause haemoglobin to release some of its oxygen more readily. These conditions are:

- a decrease in the partial pressure of oxygen in the muscle, which increases the oxygen diffusion gradient
- an increase in temperature in the blood and muscle
- an increase in carbon dioxide in the muscle, which increases the carbon dioxide diffusion gradient
- an increase in acidity (lower pH), which causes oxygen to dissociate from haemoglobin more quickly (Bohr effect)

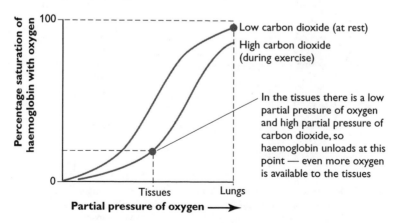

Respiratory volumes

Definitions and values of respiratory volumes, together with the way they change during exercise are given in the table below.

Lung volume or capacity	Definition	Average value at rest/dm³	Change during exercise
Tidal volume	Volume of air breathed in or out per breath	0.5	Increase
Inspiratory reserve volume	Volume of air that can be forcibly inspired after a normal breath	3.1	Decrease
Expiratory reserve volume	Volume of air that can be forcibly expired after a normal breath	1.2	Slight decrease
Residual volume	Volume of air that remains in the lungs after maximum expiration	1.2	Remains the same
Vital capacity	Volume of air forcibly expired after maximum inspiration in one breath	4.8	Remains the same
Minute ventilation	Volume of air breathed in or out per minute	6–7.5	Increases
Total lung capacity	Vital capacity + residual volume	6.0	Remains the same

Measurement of lung capacity

To measure lung capacity, an individual breathes into a spirometer, which produces a graph called a spirometer trace. Such a trace is shown in the diagram below.

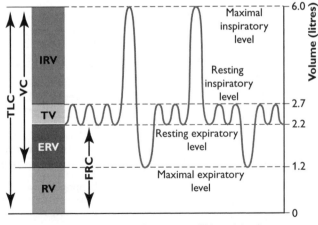

IRV = inspiratory reserve volume   TV = tidal volume
ERV = expiratory reserve volume   RV = residual volume
TLC = total lung capacity   VC = vital capacity
FRC = functional residual capacity

Control of ventilation

Breathing is controlled by the nervous system, which automatically causes an increase or decrease in the rate, depth and rhythm of breathing.

Exercise results in changes in the body that are detected by receptors:
- Chemoreceptors detect changes in blood acidity.
- Baroreceptors detect changes in blood pressure.
- Proprioceptors detect extra movement caused by exercise.
- Stretch receptors prevent over inflation of the lungs.

Impulses from chemoreceptors and baroreceptors are detected by the inspiratory cells of the respiratory centre in the medulla oblongata.

Excessive stretching results in impulses being sent to the expiratory cells of the respiratory centre in the medulla oblongata of the brain, which then sends impulses that induce expiration. This is called the Hering–Breuer reflex.

The control of ventilation is summarised in the diagram below.

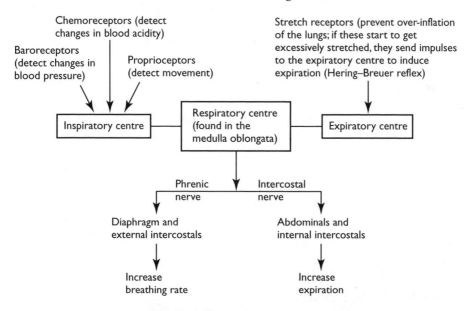

What the examiner will expect you to be able to do

- Questions on respiration often centre on how the body copes with the increased demand for oxygen caused by a raised intensity of exercise.
- You might be required to calculate specific lung volumes, so make sure you take a calculator into the exam.

The cardiovascular system
The cardiac cycle and the conduction system

The cardiac cycle

The cardiac cycle describes the emptying and filling of the heart and involves a number of stages. Systole means contraction; diastole refers to relaxation.

Atrial systole
- Atrial walls contract and blood is forced through the bicuspid and tricuspid valves into the ventricles.
- Ventricle walls relax and the ventricles fill with blood.

Ventricular systole
- Atrial walls relax — blood neither enters nor leaves the atria.
- Ventricle walls contract:
  - Initially, no blood leaves but the pressure of blood in the ventricles increases.
  - Then, the pressure of blood opens the semilunar valves and blood is ejected into the pulmonary artery and the aorta.

Diastole
- Atrial walls relax:
  - Blood enters the atria, but cannot pass into the ventricles because the tricuspid and bicuspid valves are closed.
  - Blood enters the atria and passes into the ventricles as the valves open.
- Ventricle walls relax:
  - Initially, blood neither enters nor leaves the ventricles.
  - Then, blood enters the ventricles from the atria. This is passive ventricular filling — it is *not* due to atrial contraction.

The cardiac cycle is triggered by an electrical impulse called the cardiac impulse or conduction system.

The conduction system

When the heart beats, blood flows through it in a controlled manner — in through the atria and out through the ventricles. Heart muscle is described as **myogenic** because the beat starts in the heart muscle itself, with an electrical signal in the **sinoatrial node** (SA node/pacemaker). This electrical signal then spreads through the heart in what is often described as a wave of excitation (analogy has been made to a Mexican wave).

From the SA node, the electrical signal spreads through the walls of the atria, causing them to contract and force blood into the ventricles. The signal then passes through the **atrioventricular node** (AV node) in the atrioventricular septum and down through specialised fibres called the **bundle of His**. This is located in the septum separating the two ventricles. The bundle of His branches into two bundle branches and then moves into smaller bundles called **Purkinje fibres** that spread throughout the ventricles. When the impulse passes through these fibres, it causes them to contract.

Heart rate response to exercise

Cardiac terms

- **Stroke volume** is the amount of blood pumped out by the left ventricle in each contraction. On average, the resting stroke volume is approximately 70 cm^3.
- **Heart rate** is the number of times the heart beats per minute. On average, the resting heart rate is approximately 72 beats per minute.
- **Cardiac output** is the amount of blood pumped out by *each* ventricle per minute. It is equal to stroke volume multiplied by heart rate:

$$\text{cardiac output } (Q) = \text{stroke volume } (SV) \times \text{heart rate } (HR)$$
$$= 70 \times 72 = 5040 \text{ cm}^3 \text{ (5.04 dm}^3\text{)}$$

Changes in cardiac output, stroke volume and heart rate during exercise

Regular aerobic training results in hypertrophy of the cardiac muscle, i.e. the heart physically gets bigger. This has important effects on stroke volume and heart rate, and therefore cardiac output. A bigger heart enables more blood to be pumped out per beat (i.e. increased stroke volume). In more complex language — the end diastolic volume of the ventricle increases. If the ventricle can contract with more force and push out more blood, the heart does not have to beat so often. Therefore, the resting heart rate decreases. This is called **bradycardia**. The increase in stroke volume and decrease in resting heart rate mean that cardiac output at rest remains unchanged. However, during exercise an increase in heart rate, coupled with an increase in stroke volume, results in an increase in cardiac output.

The following table shows the differences in cardiac output (to the nearest litre, i.e. dm^3) in a trained and an untrained individual at rest and during exercise. The individuals are aged 18, so their maximum heart rate is 202 beats per minute (bpm). (Maximum heart rate is calculated as 220 minus a person's age.)

Individual	Condition	SV/cm^3	HR/bpm	Q/dm^3
Untrained	Rest	70	72	5
	Exercise	120	202	24
Trained	Rest	85	60	5
	Exercise	170	202	34

This increase in cardiac output has huge benefits for trained individuals. It means that more blood, and therefore more oxygen, is transported to the working muscles. In addition, when the body starts to exercise, the distribution of blood flow changes — a higher proportion of blood passes to the working muscles and less goes to other organs.

Varying intensities of workload and recovery

The heart rate response to maximal and sub-maximal exercise and during recovery from exercise is shown on the graphs below.

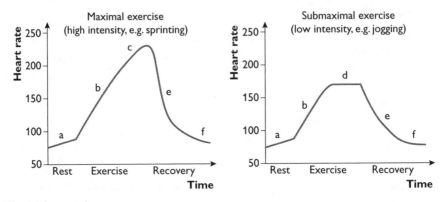

Key to the graphs:
- **a** = anticipatory rise due to the action of the hormone adrenaline
- **b** = sharp rise in heart rate, mainly due to anaerobic work
- **c** = heart rate continuing to rise due to maximal workloads stressing the anaerobic systems
- **d** = steady state as the athlete is able to meet the oxygen demand
- **e** = rapid decline in heart rate as soon as the exercise stops
- **f** = slower recovery as body systems return to resting levels

Control of blood supply

Control of heart rate

Neural control
This involves the **autonomic nervous system**:
- The **sympathetic system** stimulates the heart to beat faster.
- The **parasympathetic system** returns the heart to its resting level.

These two systems are coordinated by the **cardiac control centre** located in the medulla oblongata of the brain. The cardiac control centre is stimulated by:
- **chemoreceptors** (which detect chemical changes)
- **baroreceptors** (which detect a change in blood pressure)
- **proprioceptors** (which detect movement)

This centre then sends an impulse through either the sympathetic or parasympathetic systems to the sinoatrial node of the heart.

Hormonal control

Adrenaline and **noradrenaline** stimulate the SA node (pacemaker) and increase both the speed *and* force of muscle contraction.

Intrinsic control

During exercise, the heart becomes warmer, so heart rate increases. (A drop in temperature results in a reduced heart rate.) In addition, venous return (see page 34) increases, which stretches the cardiac muscle, stimulating the SA node. This, in turn, increases heart rate and the force of contraction. As a result, stroke volume increases.

Pulmonary and systemic circulations

- The **pulmonary circulation** sends deoxygenated blood from the heart to the lungs and returns oxygenated blood from the lungs to the heart.
- The **systemic circulation** sends oxygenated blood from the heart to the body tissues and returns deoxygenated blood from the body tissues to the heart.

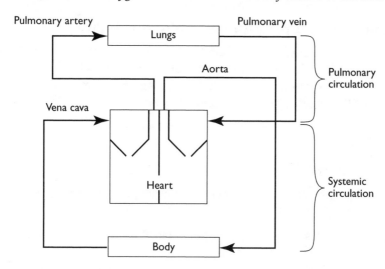

Blood vessels

The vascular system consists of five different types of blood vessel that carry the blood from the heart, distribute it round the body and return it to the heart.

Arteries carry blood away from the heart. Each heartbeat pushes blood through the arteries by a surge of pressure. The elastic arterial walls expand with each surge, which can be felt as a pulse in the arteries near the surface of the skin. The arteries then branch off and divide into smaller vessels called **arterioles**, which in turn divide into microscopic vessels called **capillaries**. A capillary wall consists of a single layer of endothelium cells. Capillaries are only wide enough to allow red blood cells to pass through one at a time. The exchange of substances with the tissues takes place across the capillary walls and the blood then flows from the capillaries to the **venules** which gradually increase in size and eventually form **veins**. To summarise, the order in which the blood flows through the vascular system is as follows:

heart ⟶ arteries ⟶ arterioles ⟶ capillaries ⟶ venules ⟶ veins ⟶ heart

Important features of arteries, capillaries and veins are summarised in the table below.

Feature	Artery	Capillary	Vein
Tunica externa — outer layer containing collagen fibres	Present	Absent	Present
Tunica media — middle layer made up of elastic fibres and smooth muscle	Thick with many elastic fibres	Absent	Thinner than in an artery
Tunica interna — inner layer made up of thin epithelial cells that are smooth to reduce friction	Present	Present	Present
Size of lumen	Small	Microscopic	Large
Valves	Absent	Absent	Present

The pulse, blood pressure and blood velocity

The **pulse** is a wave of pressure generated when the left ventricle pumps blood into the aorta. The pulse can be felt at a number of places in the body — the radial artery in the wrist and the carotid artery in the neck being the two most usual sites. Other sites include the femoral, brachial and temporal arteries.

Blood pressure is the force exerted by the blood on the blood vessel walls. It can be referred to as:

blood flow × resistance

Blood pressure is measured at the brachial artery (in the upper arm) using a sphygmo-manometer. A typical reading is: $\frac{120}{80}$ mmHg (millimetres of mercury).

Blood pressure varies in the different types of blood vessel, and is largely dependent on the distance of the blood vessel from the heart:
- **Arteries** — high in pulses
- **Arterioles** — not as high in arteries
- **Capillaries** — drops throughout the capillary network
- **Veins** — low

The smaller the cross-sectional area of a blood vessel, the higher is the blood velocity. Although the capillaries are the smallest of the blood vessels, the fact that there are so many of them means that the total cross-sectional area is much greater than that of the aorta. This means that the flow of blood is slower in the capillaries and allows enough time for efficient exchanges with the tissues. The relationship of blood velocity and cross-sectional area of the different blood vessels is highlighted in the diagram below.

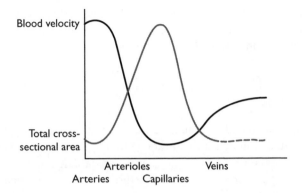

Blood velocity

Total cross-
sectional area

Arteries   Arterioles   Capillaries   Veins

Exercise and its effects on blood pressure and blood volume
- Systolic pressure rises during aerobic exercise because of an increase in cardiac output; diastolic pressure remains constant.
- During isometric work, diastolic pressure rises because of the increased resistance on blood vessels.
- A decrease in blood volume occurs during exercise when plasma moves out of the capillaries and into the surrounding tissues.
- After a period of training, blood volume increases due mainly to a rise in the volume of blood plasma and a small increase in red blood cell concentration.

Vasomotor control
The **vasomotor centre** in the medulla of the brain controls blood pressure and blood flow. The vasomotor centre is stimulated by:
- chemoreceptors, which detect chemical change
- baroreceptors, which respond to changes in blood pressure

Blood flow is then redistributed through **vasodilation** and **vasoconstriction**. Vasodilation increases blood flow; vasoconstriction decreases blood flow.

The vascular shunt
During exercise, the working muscles need more oxygen. Vasodilation of the vessels supplying muscles occurs, which increases blood flow and brings in much-needed oxygen. At the same time, vasoconstriction occurs in the arterioles supplying non-essential organs. This redirection of blood flow is called the **vascular shunt**.

Pre-capillary sphincters also aid blood redistribution. These are tiny rings of muscle located at the openings of capillaries. When they contract, the blood flow through the capillaries is restricted; when they relax, blood flow is increased. During exercise, the capillary networks supplying skeletal muscle have relaxed pre-capillary sphincters. Therefore, the blood flow to the muscles is increased and the tissues are saturated with oxygen.

Re-directing blood flow (cardiac output) has huge benefits for trained athletes, because more blood, and therefore more oxygen, is transported to the working muscles. In addition, when the body starts to exercise, the distribution of blood flow changes.

This means that a much higher proportion of blood passes to the working muscles and less passes to organs such as the intestine. The amount of blood passing to the kidneys and brain remains unaltered.

Venous return

This is the term used for blood that is returned to the right-hand side of the heart through the veins.

At rest, 70% of the total blood volume is contained in the veins. This provides a large reservoir of blood that can be returned rapidly to the heart when needed. The heart can only pump out as much blood as it receives, so cardiac output is dependent on venous return. A rapid increase in venous return enables a significant increase in stroke volume and, therefore, cardiac output. Veins have a large lumen and offer little resistance to blood flow. By the time that blood enters the veins, blood pressure is low. This means that active mechanisms are needed to ensure venous return:

- **Skeletal muscle pump** — when muscles contract and relax they change shape. This change in shape means that the muscles press on nearby veins, causing a pumping effect and squeezing the blood towards the heart.
- **Respiratory pump** — when muscles contract and relax during inspiration and expiration, pressure changes occur in the thoracic and abdominal cavities. These pressure changes compress the nearby veins and enable blood to return to the heart.
- **Valves** — it is important that blood in the veins flows in only one direction. The presence of valves ensures that this happens. This is because once the blood has passed through a valve, the valve closes, preventing the blood from flowing back.

In addition, **gravity** assists the flow of blood from body parts above the heart.

Effects of training

The effects of training on lung volumes, lung capacities and gaseous exchange

Endurance training causes an increase in the inspiratory and expiratory reserve volumes and, therefore, vital capacity.

The exchange of gases at the alveoli becomes more efficient. This is because training causes an increase in the surface area and, in addition, there is an increased density of the surrounding capillaries. This means that more oxygen diffuses into the blood from the lungs and reaches the working muscles efficiently. Similarly, waste products are dealt with more effectively.

Effects of training on cardiac function

The effects of training on cardiac function include **athlete's heart**, which is the common term for an enlarged heart caused by repeated strenuous exercise. Due to the increased demands of exercise the chambers of the heart enlarge, as does muscle mass (**hypertrophy**). This results in an increase in the volume of blood that can be pumped out per beat, i.e. a rise in **stroke volume** and maximum **cardiac output**. Consequently, the heart has to contract less frequently and there is a decrease in resting heart rate (**bradycardia**).

What the examiner will expect you to be able to do

- You should learn the structures involved in the cardiovascular system. You will be expected to be able to relate these structures to exercise — for example, how the cardiovascular system functions to ensure the blood supply is maintained during exercise.
- Make sure that you are aware of how training can improve performance. Physiological adaptations take place after a period of time, and will make initial training sessions appear very easy. This is because more oxygen can be taken in, transported and utilised by the muscle cells.

Defining, developing and classifying skills

A skilful performance has the following characteristics:
- **learned** — practice of a skill 'makes perfect'
- **efficient and economical** — minimum outlay of time and energy
- **goal-directed** — pre-determined results
- **follows a technical model** — a perfect demonstration of coaching points
- **consistent** — maximum certainty of success
- **fluent** — movements flow together
- **aesthetic** — pleasing to the eye

The types of skill that are important in PE are:
- **cognitive** — a skill involving the mental or intellectual ability of the performer (e.g. tactically outwitting an opponent in a long-distance race)
- **perceptual** — a skill involving the detection and interpretation of information (e.g. deciding where to pass the ball in soccer or if weather conditions might affect play)
- **motor** — a skill that involves movement and muscular control (e.g. swimming lengths)
- **perceptual/psychomotor** — this involves the cognitive, perceptual and motor aspects of skill (e.g. in a match situation, deciding who to pass to in soccer, and when and where to make the pass, and then actually making the pass)

Analysis of movement skills

Movement skills usually have several parts that are referred to as sub-routines. For example, in the front crawl swimming stroke, the sub-routines are body position, arm action, leg action and breathing.

A **continuum** (plural continua) is an imaginary scale between two extremes to show a gradual increase or decrease in characteristic. There are six continua you need to know and understand so that you can then apply them practically in order to classify different sports skills.

Continua used to classify skills

The four continua used to classify skills are:
- **environmental influence** — open–closed
- **pacing** — external–self
- **continuity** — discrete–serial–continuous
- **muscular involvement** — gross–fine

Environmental influence

Movement skills are affected by an **open environment** because the environment is always changing (e.g. the positions of opponents and team mates). There is much instant decision making (e.g. in invasion game situations). Skills are usually externally paced and are not predominantly habitual.

In a **closed environment**, skills are unaffected by the environment, which is predictable. They are habitual and follow a precise, well-practised technical model (e.g. a vault in gymnastics). They are usually self-paced, i.e. the performer has control.

Pacing

If a movement is **self-paced**, the performer is in control and determines when the movement starts and the rate at which it proceeds (e.g. a free throw in basketball).

If a movement is **externally paced**, control of the movement is not determined by the performer but by the environment (e.g. by the opponent(s), when passing in basketball).

Continuity

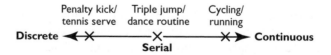

Discrete skills have a clear, distinct beginning and end. To be repeated, the skill must be started again (e.g. taking a penalty kick in football and rugby).

Serial skills have several discrete elements that are put together in a particular order to make a sequence or compound skill (e.g. the triple jump or a floor routine in gymnastics)

Continuous skills have no clear beginning or end. The same skill or movement is repeated (e.g. cycling).

Muscular involvement

Gross ← Shot put/ rugby tackle — Darts/ pistol shot → Fine

Gross motor skills involve the movement of large muscles (e.g. shot put and weight-lifting).

Fine motor skills involve precise, intricate movements using small muscle groups. The emphasis is on hand–eye coordination (e.g. darts).

Examples of continua used to classify skills

A **javelin throw** is:
- closed, because the environment does not change
- self-paced, because the athlete starts when ready
- gross, because it is an explosive movement and rest is required between throws
- discrete, because it has a clear beginning and an end

A **swimming race start** is:
- discrete, because it has a clear, distinct beginning and an end
- externally paced, because swimmers react to the stimulus of the gun
- a whole skill, because it cannot be broken down into sub-parts
- closed, because only one response movement is appropriate to the single stimulus presented. The environment is therefore constant.

The application of classification of skills in the organisation and determination of practice

Classifying skills helps PE teachers and coaches, because it tells them how to:
- teach skills
- improve skills
- practise skills to optimise performance

Before deciding on the type of practice, the coach or teacher should first classify the skill. Does the skill to be learned contain:
- several integrated actions? If so, it is a serial skill.
- a single integrated action? If so, it is a discrete skill.
- cyclical action? If so, it is a continuous skill.
- perceptual requirements? If so, it is an open skill.
- stereotyped movements? If so, it is a closed skill because the environment is constant/unchanged

The teacher or coach then has to decide how to organise practice. Does the movement to be learned involve:
- skills that can be broken into parts? If so, it is a low-organisation skill.
- skills that cannot be broken into separate parts? If so, it is a high organisation skill.
- fine, intricate and perceptual skills? If so, it is a complex skill.
- gross, habitual or ballistic skills? If so, it is a simple skill.

Practice types and key terms explained in relation to sporting examples

Varied practice

In varied practice, the environment is continually changing. Therefore, varied practice is best for open skills. An example is three-versus-one 'keep ball' in netball or football.

Points about varied practice include the following:
- It improves positional play and passing technique in a realistic game situation.
- Opportunities arise for decision-making and the development of perceptual skills.
- Performers learn to adapt techniques to respond to an ever-changing environment.
- Adaptations are stored and, therefore, the experience (or schema) of the novice performer is expanded.
- It improves selective attention. This is the ability to pick out and focus on relevant parts of the display.
- It develops the skill of detecting warning signals (the cues before the major environmental ones), making information processing (the decision-making process) faster and more efficient.

Fixed practice

In fixed practice, the skills performed remain the same or repetitive. The environment does not change. Fixed practice is best for 'closed skills' that need to be 'over-learned' and well grooved (e.g. how to vault in gymnastics, skill drills or repetitive practices).

Fixed practice can be used because:
- the environment in which a closed skill is performed remains the same
- once perfected, the movement pattern does not change

Body movements that never change are known as **stereotyped actions**. They should be well grooved to the point at which they become habitual.

Part practice

For more complex movements, part practice allows confidence, motivation and understanding to build up gradually. Part practice involves working on an isolated sub-routine to try to perfect it. It is best for skills that are low in organisation, and which can be broken down easily into separate sub-routines.

Points about part practice include the following:
- It can reduce fatigue in physically demanding skills. For example, the throwing phase in discus could be the focus of teaching and allow the learner to concentrate on this one area.
- It is useful in reducing overload (e.g. for a novice performer).
- It is useful when a task is complex or dangerous.
- Some skills can be taught by reversing the part order. For example, for shot put, the order of teaching would be:
  - throw and release
  - travel and trunk position
  - initial preparation
  - stance
  - grip
  This is called **backward chaining**.

Whole practice

Whole practice is best for skills that are high in organisation. An example is dribbling a ball in hockey. This does not easily break down into separate sub-routines.

Some points about whole practice include the following:
- It is the ideal model for all movements as it allows the learner to experience the feel of the skill (kinaesthesis).
- It is best for simple, discrete skills where a single, complete action is required.
- It wastes no time in assembling parts.
- Transfer to 'real situations' from practice is likely to be positive.

Whole–part–whole practice

Whole–part–whole practice allows the performer to get the feel of the movement. Using swimming as an example:
- This type of practice initially involves the presentation of the whole motor programme, i.e. an entire swimming stroke.
- Then, by introducing a float as a mechanical aid, practice focuses on a part of the skill, such as the leg kick.
- Finally, the whole stroke is reintroduced. The leg kick should have improved as a result of isolating it, giving relevant drills, teaching points and feedback to swimmers.

Ability and how it differs from skill

The words 'skill' and 'ability' are often used to mean the same thing. However, they are different terms with different characteristics.

Abilities are:
- innate, stable and enduring qualities that support many skills
- general — not specific

The characteristics of skill and ability are summarised in the table below.

Characteristic of skill	Characteristic of ability	Explanation
A movement that is learned	Innate (inherited)	Inborn abilities are determined by the genes inherited from our parents
Can be modified with practice	Stable, enduring proficiency	Abilities tend to remain unchanged
Depends on several abilities	Supports many skills	Each skill usually needs several supporting abilities in order to be well-learned

Tip Condensing information into a table can be an effective method of revision.

Types of ability

You need to understand and be able to give examples of two types of ability:
- **Gross motor abilities** involve physical proficiency abilities or movements and link to physical fitness. For example, explosive strength involves the effective use of energy for a short burst of effort, as in a rugby union tackle or line-out jump.
- **Perceptual** or **psychomotor abilities** involve information processing and decision making and then putting these decisions into action via movements. For example, being able to make rapid arm and hand movements that involve objects at speed, such as catching a ball as a slip fielder in cricket.

What the examiner will expect you to be able to do

- The difference between skill and ability is often asked in examination questions. You will be expected to be able to identify the supporting or 'underpinning' abilities for different activities. For example, gymnasts need strength, balance, coordination and flexibility. The questions sometimes ask for explanations of how abilities are developed during childhood. Possibilities include giving children a wide range of experiences and opportunities to practise, while receiving expert teaching or coaching.
- You will be expected to apply knowledge of different practice conditions to practical sporting examples and stages of learning.
- You should ensure you know at least *three* different characteristics of skill (e.g. consistent, learned and aesthetic).
- If you are asked to 'classify a skill', it is important that you can *explain* and *justify* how you have arrived at your decision. This is because the skill will differ depending on the situation in which it is performed. You will be required to explain this, together with characteristics of the skill that are relevant to the classification system you have chosen.

> • Make sure that you can list and explain the key characteristics of skilful performers. Relating them to your favourite sporting activity might help you to remember them.

Information processing during performance

Key processes in information processing

The improvement in performance of a skill can be related to various key processes involved in information processing. In order, these are:

display $\longrightarrow$ sensory $\longrightarrow$ perception $\longrightarrow$ memory $\longrightarrow$ decision making $\longrightarrow$ effector mechanism $\longrightarrow$ feedback

- **Display** — the surroundings or environment of the performer. For example, for a footballer, display includes the ball, team mates, opponents, spectators, the referee and the coach or teacher.
- **Sensory input** — the senses detect information and receptors are stimulated. The senses involved are vision, hearing and **proprioception**. Proprioception is the sense that allows us to know the position of our bodies and what our muscles and joints are doing, and to feel objects involved in our performance (e.g. the ball or hockey stick). Proprioceptive sense consists of **touch**, **kinaesthesis** and **equilibrium**.
- **Perception** — the process that interprets and makes sense of the information received. It consists of three elements:
  - **detection** — detecting that the stimulus is present
  - **comparison** — comparing the stimulus to stimuli present in the long-term memory
  - **recognition** — matching the stimulus to one found in long-term memory
- **Memory** — important in both perceptual and decision-making processes. It consists of **short-term sensory stores** (STSS), **short-term memory** (STM) and **long-term memory** (LTM). (See page 44 for further explanation of these terms.)
- **Decision making** — the translatory mechanism. Once the information has been interpreted, the correct response has to be put into action. This will be in the form of a **motor programme**.
- **Effector mechanism** — the motor programme is put into action by sending impulses through the nervous system to the appropriate muscles, enabling them to carry out the required actions.
- **Feedback** — once the motor programme has been put into action, the display changes and new information is created. This new information is known as feedback.

It is important to show that you understand terms such as perception, translation (decision-making) and effective control by being able to link them with appropriate sporting activities.

For example, in volleyball:

- **perception** involves making sense of incoming information, i.e. using selective attention in order to see the stimulus of the ball leaving the hand of the opposing server.
- **translation** — deciding what is happening and what action to take through the interaction of short-term and long-term memory. For example: 'with the ball at chest height, I will use a set volley'.
- **effector control** — carrying out the movement (e.g. hands high, 'viewfinder').

Models of information processing

Whiting's model of information processing for perceptual motor performance

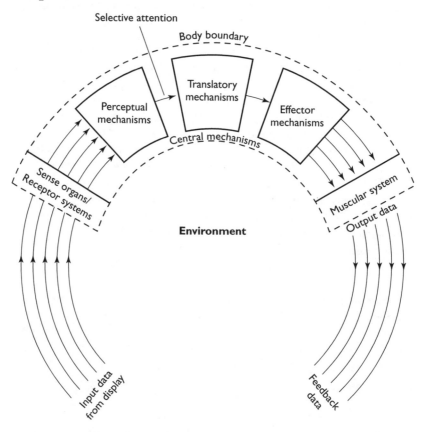

An important point to note about this model is that it shows five arrows entering the perceptual mechanism and only one leaving. This process is called **selective attention**. It allows unnecessary information to be filtered out and helps us to focus on relevant information in a system of 'limited capacity'.

Other points to note are as follows:

- Input comes from the display, i.e. the sporting environment.
- Specific parts of the display stimulate the sense organs and, therefore, pass to the receptors.
- The translatory mechanisms recognise the input and decisions are made about what action to take.
- The effector mechanisms send impulses to the muscular system so that the movement can be carried out.
- An action is performed (output data).
- Feedback is required for accurate performance.

Welford's model of information processing

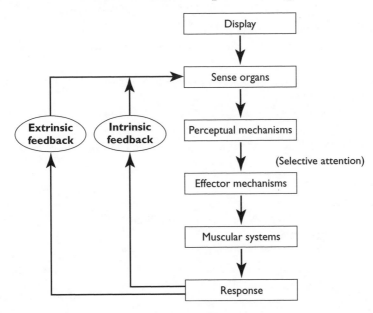

According to this model:

- **display** is the sporting environment from which information is selected.
- **sense organs** are responsible for picking up important information from the display.
- **perceptual mechanisms** decide on the appropriate response.
- **effector mechanisms and muscular systems** carry out movements once decisions have been made.
- **extrinsic feedback** is feedback from a source outside the performer.
- **intrinsic feedback** is feedback from within the performer.

The memory process

Memory is important in:

- storing and retrieving information
- interpreting information by comparing it with that from a previous experience
- determining the motor programme to use to implement the action

Components of memory

Short-term sensory store

The features of the short-term sensory store (STSS) are as follows:

- All information is held for a very short time (0.25–1 second).
- Capacity is limitless within the brief time available.
- Important information is attended to (selective attention); that which is not important is ignored and eventually lost and replaced by new information.
- The perceptual mechanism determines important information (recognition aspect of perception).
- Input from the STSS goes into the short-term memory (STM).

Short-term memory

Short-term memory (STM) is referred to as **working memory**. The features of STM are as follows:

- Information is compared with that which has been previously learned (comparison aspect of perception).
- Information is only stored for up to a minute or so, unless it is rehearsed or repeated.
- It has limited capacity — 7±2 pieces of information.
- Capacity can be increased by '**chunking**' with other information (see page 45).
- It is responsible for the execution of the motor programme.

Long-term memory

The features of long-term memory (LTM) are as follows:

- It stores information that has been well-learned and practised.
- It has a very large/unlimited capacity.
- After much practise, motor programmes are stored in the LTM.
- Stored information is retrieved and compared with new information — this is the recognition aspect of perception.

Strategies to improve retention and retrieval

There are a number of strategies that can be applied to help store and remember information:

- **Rehearsal and practice** — frequently practising and rehearsing the skill stores the motor programme. It also creates a memory trace, by carrying the skill image to-and-fro between the short-term and long-term memories.
- **Association/linking** — linking new information with that already known. For example, the sports-specific skill of catching a cricket ball is linked to the fundamental motor skill of catching.

- **Simplicity** — learners should be allowed time to take in new information, which should be kept as simple as possible. More complex details can be added later. Similar types of information or skill should not be presented too close together. For example, a swimming teacher should concentrate on one stroke at a time.
- **Organisation** — information should be organised and presented in a meaningful way. For example, a gymnastic or trampolining sequence should be learned by practising the individual movements in the order in which they appear.
- **Chunking** — linking information together allows more information to be dealt with at the same time. Experienced performers can look at the whole field of play. Coaches should avoid giving too much information at a time, particularly to inexperienced performers.
- **Uniqueness** — presenting information in an unusual way makes it more likely to be remembered.
- **Positive reinforcement** — if learners receive praise and encouragement, the information is more likely to be remembered. This requires frequent feedback.
- **Interesting/enjoyable** — if learners enjoy the experience, the possibility of it being remembered increases.
- **Meaningful** — if learners appreciate the relevance of the skill to their performance, they are more likely to remember it.
- **Imagery** — if learners have a mental image of the skill, they are more likely to remember it. This is why demonstrations are important.

Tip To help you remember the above, it would be a good idea to convert this information into another format, such as a spider diagram, with links to practical examples.

Reaction time

Key terms

- **Reaction time** is the time from the stimulus occurring to the performer starting to move in response to it
- **Movement time** is the time taken from starting the movement to completing it
- **Response time** is the time from the onset of the stimulus to the completion of the movement

Using the 100 metres sprint as an example:

starter's gun goes off ⟶ sprinter pushes on blocks = reaction time
sprinter pushing on blocks ⟶ sprinter crossing finish line = movement time
starter's gun goes off ⟶ sprinter crosses finish line = response time

A further sporting example to aid your understanding of reaction time, movement time and response time can be taken from tennis. Top-class professional tennis players serve at very high speeds. Suppose that it takes:

- 0.17 seconds for the ball to reach the receiver once it has left the server's racket
- 0.15 seconds for the receiver to decide on an action
- 0.20 seconds for the receiver to play a return, having decided on the stroke to play

From these data, the receiver's reaction, movement and response times can be calculated as:

reaction time = 0.15 seconds
movement time = 0.20 seconds
response time = 0.35 seconds

Factors affecting reaction time

There are a number of factors that affect reaction time. They include:
- the **sensory system** used — kinaesthesis is quickest, sight slowest
- the **limb** used — feet are slower than hands and the preferred side is usually quicker
- **personality** — extroverts react more quickly than introverts

Reaction time can also be affected by external factors, including:
- a warning. If a warning is given, it helps to prepare the athlete. An example is 'set' at the start of a sprint.
- the intensity of stimulus. For example, using an orange ball when playing football in the snow helps players to pick it out from the background.
- the likelihood of the stimulus occurring. If the stimulus has a good chance of happening, the reaction will be quicker.

Simple and choice reaction times

Simple reaction time is the time taken for a sports performer to react to a **single stimulus**.

Choice reaction time occurs when there is more than one stimulus and/or more than one response. It occurs in many sporting situations. When there are more choices and decisions to be made, reaction times lengthen.

Hicks's law

Hicks's law states that choice reaction time *increases linearly* with the number of stimulus and choice alternatives. For example, if there is double the choice, the reaction time doubles.

Hicks's law has important implications for sports performers, who should try to:
- disguise their intentions, therefore increasing the number of possible alternatives that opponents have to select from. This increases the reaction times of the opponents.
- pick up 'cues' about the intended response of their opponents. This reduces the number of alternatives and reaction times are reduced.

Ways to improve the response time of a performer

There are a number of ways in which teachers and coaches can try to improve the response time of a performer. These include:
- practising responses to a stimulus (e.g. sprint starts to a 'gun')

- using mental rehearsal to help performers attend to correct cues
- ensuring optimum level of arousal
- making sure that the cardiorespiratory and neuromuscular systems are adequately prepared
- developing 'predictive skills' (e.g. anticipating a slower delivery in cricket)

Psychological refractory period

This is the negative side of anticipation. If we anticipate something wrongly, then our reactions are slower. If we detect a stimulus and are processing that information when a second stimulus arrives, we cannot attend to the second stimulus until we have finished processing the first. Therefore, humans can only deal with one piece of information at a time (the single-channel hypothesis). This delay in processing information increases reaction time. The delay is called the **psychological refractory period** (PRP).

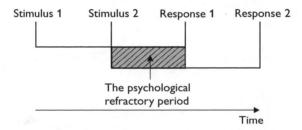

The PRP is the delay caused by being able to process only one piece of information at a time. An example of its importance is in games such as rugby, when 'dummying' an opponent. An opponent who 'buys the dummy' is still reacting to it when the second stimulus of carrying on without releasing the ball is received. Deception makes use of the PRP by creating uncertainty and insecurity in sports performers.

Feedback

Feedback is the information received by the performer during the course of the movement or as a result of it. There are several different types of feedback of which you need to be aware. These are summarised in the tables below:

Intrinsic feedback	Extrinsic feedback
Comes from within (e.g. proprioceptors and kinaesthesis)	Comes from external sources (e.g. teacher or coach)
Concerns the feel of the movement (e.g. the feel of balance during a handstand)	Received via sight and hearing and is used to support intrinsic feedback
Very important for experienced performers	Important for beginners who are often reliant on it if they wish to improve
Novices need to be made aware of the need to develop this form of feedback	

Concurrent (continuous) feedback	Terminal feedback
Intrinsic	Extrinsic
Received during the movement and generated by the proprioceptors or kinaesthesis (e.g. gymnasts knowing they are balanced correctly)	Given after the movement is completed or later (e.g. a coach discussing the match and summarising the performance at the next training session)

Positive feedback	Negative feedback
Movement is successful and feedback reinforces the learning	Movement is incorrect or unsuccessful and feedback is used to make it successful (i.e. error correction)
Can be intrinsic or extrinsic (e.g. positive extrinsic feedback is when a badminton coach praises players when they serve correctly): this can motivate the performers to succeed	Can be intrinsic or extrinsic (e.g. negative intrinsic feedback is when advanced-level performers detect or 'feel' an error in movement and then try to correct it themselves)

Knowledge of performance (KP)	Knowledge of results (KR)
Concerns the quality of movement	Concerns the outcome of movement
Could be from discussing the performance or watching a video	Usually arises from teachers or coaches seeing the result (e.g. from watching the movement on video
Can be external (from teachers or coaches) or internal (from proprioceptors and kinaesthesis)	Extrinsic Can be positive or negative
Important for experienced performers	Very important in the early stages of learning and for improving performance

Why is feedback important?

Feedback is important because:
- performers know what to do in order to improve
- correct actions are reinforced
- incorrect actions are stopped and bad habits are prevented
- performers are motivated and their confidence is boosted

In order for feedback to be effective, it should:
- make comparisons with previous performances
- be specific to the performance
- be easily understood
- be in manageable amounts
- be linked to goals
- be immediate, so that it remains firmly in the memory

What the examiner will expect you to be able to do

- Questions may require you to explain how feedback differs as performers move through the stages of learning, i.e. from the associative phase to the autonomous phase:
  - At the associative phase, performers begin to monitor their own feedback, but extrinsic feedback from a coach is still needed.
  - At the autonomous phase, performers become less reliant on KR (knowledge of results), and are better at detecting their own errors through intrinsic feedback. Performers are able to correct their own performance.
- Questions on information processing are often about one of the information-processing models. A useful approach is to try to draw the model or use the diagram provided to explain each part sequentially. Practical examples to illustrate your understanding should be used at each stage.
- Questions on the memory process may require you to name some of the features of the various storage parts of the memory. For example, the long-term memory is said to have limitless capacity, to last a lifetime and to store motor programmes. It is important to read the questions carefully and give accurate answers (e.g. make sure that you do not confuse the short-term sensory store with the short-term memory).
- You need to be able to define reaction time, movement time and response time and relate these to sporting examples. These are regularly asked for in the examination.
- Feedback is referred to as 'an aid to performance' and you are often asked to 'state its benefits'. Answers should include building confidence, providing motivation and correcting errors.

Control of motor skills

Motor programmes

A motor programme is a set of movements stored in the long-term memory, which specifies the components of a skill.

Key points

- Motor skills are physical actions.
- Control involves the manipulation and adjustment of movement to produce the required skill.
- A motor programme or executive motor programme (EMP) is an overall plan of the whole skill or pattern of movement.

- The plan is stored in the long-term memory (LTM).
- The EMP comprises sub-routines — mini skills often performed in sequence, which, collectively, make up the whole skill.
- Sub-routines appear to be performed fluently and automatically when the skill has been grooved or over-learned.
- Automatic execution of the skill takes place when the performer is at the expert stage.
- An expert is said to be at the autonomous phase of learning.

The organisation of a skill can be **hierarchical** and **sequential**. Hierarchical means in order of importance — the EMP is more important than the supporting sub-routines. Sequential means that sub-routines are often performed in a particular order. In the diagram below this is applied to a tennis serve, which is low in organisation. Note how the sub-routines are performed in sequence to make up the EMP.

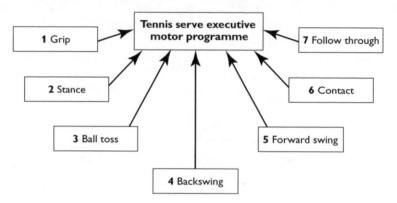

Low-organisation skills

If a skill is low in organisation (e.g. throwing the javelin), it can be divided easily into sub-routines that can be taught and practised separately.

You need to know three practice methods that can be used for a skill of low organisation. These are:

- **part practice** — each sub-routine is learned separately and in isolation
- **progressive part practice** — two sub-routines are taught separately and then practised together before teaching a third sub-routine in isolation. The combination of three sub-routines is then practised as one skill.
- **whole–part–whole** — the skill is practised as a whole. One sub-routine is taken out and practised separately. The skill is then performed as a whole.

Sub-routines, particularly in throwing skills, can often be taught in reverse order. This practice method is called **backward chaining**.

High-organisation skills

If a skill is high in organisation, it cannot be divided into sub-routines. A single sub-routine cannot be taught as an isolated component.

You need to know two practice methods that can be used for a skill of high organisation. These are:

- **whole practice** — the skill is performed as a whole (e.g. dribbling a football)
- **task simplification** — making the task easier than it really is. For example, short tennis simplifies the rudiments of the major game of tennis.

Motor control

Motor control involves manipulation and often adjustment of the body during perform-ance in order to bring about the desired response. The control of motor skills is explained by the **open-loop** and **closed-loop** theories.

Open-loop and closed-loop control (Adams)

Motor control occurs at three levels.

Level 1: open-loop control

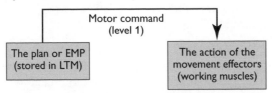

Note that open-loop control does not involve feedback.

Key points about level 1

- The EMP is stored as an overall plan in the long-term memory.
- The EMP is triggered by the 'situation' and is transferred almost spontaneously to the working muscle.
- The open loop is termed the **memory trace** and is responsible for starting the action.
- The function is to produce the initial movement of the skill and no reference is made to feedback.
- For a skill of rapid execution, such as a golf drive, the movement is so rapid that feedback cannot be referenced after the swing has started.

Levels 2 and 3: closed-loop control

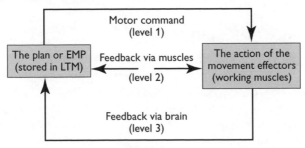

Note that levels 2 and 3 involve feedback. Feedback completes or closes the loop.

Key points about level 2
- It operates on a short feedback loop and is a closed loop system of control.
- Control is achieved through muscle reaction.
- Without thinking, rapid adjustments can be made during performance. For example, gymnasts make subconscious alterations in order to retain balance during their routines.
- Adjustments are stored in the long-term memory.
- It does not engage the central cognitive process.
- Its function is to complete the skill.

Key points about level 3
- It operates on a longer feedback loop because information is relayed to the brain, which in turn processes modifications to performance.
- Feedback is information about the performance and outcome of the skill.
- It involves thought and greater attention is given to the plan.
- Adjustments are stored in the long-term memory as fresh motor programmes.
- It is called the **perceptual trace** and is frequently used in open skills that require decision making (e.g. passing a ball in netball or hockey).
- Its function is to complete the skill.

Perceptual trace
During performance, the perceptual trace compares the current action with the learned pattern of movement, which is stored in the long-term memory. If the comparison matches, the skill is allowed to continue and is reinforced. If a mismatch is detected, the action will be modified. Modifications are stored as fresh motor programmes.

Drawbacks of open-loop and closed-loop theories
- It is not possible to store the large number of motor programmes as separate memory traces for every movement in long-term memory. This gives an information retention problem.
- If it was possible to retain an infinite number of motor programmes, it would be difficult for the memory trace to retrieve or recall the required plan in sufficient time to execute the skill.
- Sport contains many unusual/spontaneous actions. These are creative actions we often see in 'open skills' and are called 'novel responses'. If the relevant motor programme has not been set up in long-term memory, the action of the novel response cannot be explained by this theory.

Schema theory (Schmidt)

Schema theory provides a solution to the problems of the open-loop and closed-loop theories. It states that EMPs are not stored as separate plans (as presented by open-loop and closed-loop theories), but are stored in the long-term memory as experiences or relationships with motor programmes or movements. These relationships are termed 'generalised movements' and they allow performers to adapt quickly in response to a given situation.

Key points
- A schema is an accumulation of experiences.
- Stored information helps in decision making.
- Experiences or relationships are termed generalised movements.
- Generalised movements are adaptations or modifications of movements that are transferred to aid learning and performance of other skills.
- Experience can be adapted and used to meet the demands of a new situation.
- The process of using previous experience to assist with learning new skills, and with the performance of over-learned skills, is called 'transfer'.
- Schema theory supports variability of practice.

Experience is accumulated by gathering information from four sources of information or memory items. Using the example of two attackers approaching one defender in rugby, these memory items are identified and explained in the table below. The example relates *specifically* to the ball carrier.

Type of schema	Functions	Memory items stored each time a movement is performed	Explanation of memory items using a practical example
Recall	To store information	(1) Knowledge of initial conditions and desired outcome	Refers to the environmental situation (e.g. the player may have experienced a similar situation in a practice or previous game)
	To start the response	(2) Knowledge of response specification	Refers to knowing what to do (e.g. the well-timed pass may be the answer as it has been successful in similar situations)
Recognition	To control the movement	(3) Knowledge of sensory consequences (actual feedback)	Refers to kinaesthesis — how much pressure or force to apply to the skill (e.g. how hard the ball should be passed)
	To evaluate the performance	(4) Knowledge of outcome/KR	Refers to knowing what the result is likely to be (e.g. the well-timed pass makes it impossible for the defender to make a tackle. What was the result?)

Ways in which coaches can organise practices to enable schemata to develop include the following:
- Training should be varied and should:
  - include lots of information
  - be as realistic as possible (e.g. game situations)
  - include transferable elements
  - include lots of feedback
- Terminal feedback should be provided to strengthen the schema in the memory.

The relationship between learning and performance

- **Learning** is the process of producing relatively permanent changes in behaviour as a result of practice.
- **Performance** is a demonstration of the ability to carry out a given task at a given time.

Learning curves

A learning curve has three elements:
- the *y*-axis (vertical axis), which represents the measure of performance
- the *x*-axis (horizontal axis), which represents the amount of time over which the performance has been measured
- the shape of the curve, which indicates the learning that has taken place

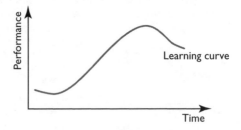

Examples of learning curves

Positive acceleration

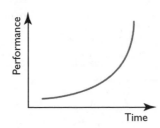

Features to note are:
- small improvements in performance in the early stages of learning
- rapid improvements in performance later

Negative acceleration

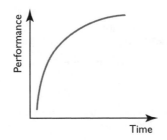

Features to note are:
- a large increase in the early stages of learning
- improvement levels off later

Linear curve

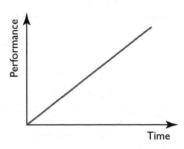

The important feature here is that performance improves proportionately with time.

S-shaped curve

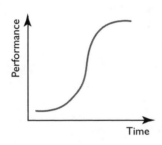

Features to note are:
- slow start to learning
- steady improvement
- levelling off in the later stages

A novice in the associative stage of learning completing a simple closed skill

A learning curve for a novice in the associative stage of learning completing a simple, closed skill, such as a tennis serve or a penalty kick, is shown below.

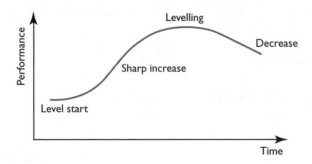

Features to note are:
- The graph starts at a low level because the novice has a low skill level.
- Early practice produces a sharp increase in performance level.
- The upper level is reached due to optimum performance or decrease in motivation.

- The levelling out (plateau) of performance may occur because of:
  - fatigue, loss of motivation or a reduction in drive level
  - poor coaching or lack of information on how to improve skill level
- The fall in performance may be due to lack of motivation, boredom, fatigue, distraction or faulty technique.

The learning plateau

A **learning plateau** occurs when there is no apparent improvement in performance. It was first thought that on reaching a learning plateau, the learner was consolidating acquired skills or knowledge. However, subsequent research does not support this belief.

Factors that contribute to a learning plateau include:
- fatigue
- loss of motivation or interest
- bad technique (negative learning)
- focusing on wrong cues
- emotions
- physical unreadiness
- low aspiration levels
- lack of ability to adapt skills

Ways in which a coach could combat the plateau effect (performance decrement) include:
- breaking the practice into shorter, distributed periods
- re-setting the goals, with the agreement of the performer
- offering extrinsic rewards and encouragement
- using mental rehearsal in practice
- giving appropriate feedback on technique and results
- ensuring competition against others of similar ability
- breaking a serial skill into its component parts (e.g. whole–part–whole practice)
- diverting the performer's attention to appropriate cues
- changing the performer's role in the team (e.g. captaincy or position)

Teaching styles

Mosston's spectrum of teaching styles

Teaching and learning involve making decisions on:
- what to teach and learn
- when to teach and learn
- how to teach and learn

This model suggests a scale of teaching styles with the teacher making the decisions at one end of the spectrum and the learner making the decisions at the other end.

There is a range of teaching styles in between that involve both the teacher and the learner in decision making.

Style 1: command
Advantages of the command style of teaching
- It is safe — the teacher is in control.
- It is disciplined.
- It is quick.
- It is good for large groups and for uniformity.
- The learner knows exactly what is required.
- It is good for dangerous activities.

Disadvantages of the command style of learning
- It discourages creativity.
- It may be boring and de-motivating.
- Poor teaching could result in bad habits.
- It can lead to poor self-discipline.
- It does not promote personal growth and may cause a lack of self-actualisation.
- The pupil becomes a model of the teacher.

Style 2: reciprocal
In the reciprocal style of teaching, pupils are taught and then teach others. Pupils become 'doers' and 'observers'. The teacher helps the 'observers', who then teach the 'doers'.

Advantages of the reciprocal style of teaching
- It gives the learner a large amount of immediate feedback.
- It is useful with large groups.
- It encourages decision making.
- It encourages interaction.

Disadvantages of the reciprocal style of teaching
- Pupils might not fully understand and then teach others the skill incorrectly.
- Teaching incorrectly can develop faulty technique.

Style 3: problem solving
In problem solving, learners have to find their own solutions in their own way. This is learning through investigation and discovery. The teacher sets open-ended questions to which the answers must be correct.

Advantages of problem solving
- It gives a sense of responsibility for one's own learning.
- It improves self-confidence and motivation.
- It encourages creativity.
- It aids self-fulfilment and self-actualisation.
- In small classes, it allows the teacher to give individual feedback.
- It is good for high-level performers.

Disadvantages of problem solving

- It is not good in the early stages of learning because pupils do not have enough knowledge with which to work.
- There may be negative safety implications, particularly with beginners or large classes.
- Individual feedback is more difficult in large classes.

Style 4: discovery

In the discovery method of teaching, pupils have to find the single solution to a problem set by the teacher.

An advantage of the discovery method is that it can be enjoyable because of its pupil-led nature.

Disadvantages of the discovery method

- The teacher may not have considered all the possible solutions.
- Trial and error can be time consuming.

What the examiner will expect you to be able to do

- You need to be able to differentiate between the benefits of a motor programme, in terms of the efficient, quick reactions it can produce, and the ways in which it is developed through feedback and practice. You could be asked to name some sub-routines of a skill and to explain how a basic motor programme can develop into a more complex one by fine-tuning the performance through specific practice.
- A question on closed-loop control will require you to use a sporting example to help explain how errors are detected and amended by feedback.
- You will be expected to know the four parts of the schema theory so that you can recall and apply them to sporting examples in any questions set on this topic area.
- You should be able to recognise and interpret the various shapes of performance curve and to relate performance plateaux to possible causes and solutions.

Learning skills
Theories related to learning movement skills

Connectionist or associationist theories

Connectionist theories depend upon linking (connecting) a **stimulus** to a **response**. This connection is often termed a **learning bond** or **S–R bond**, where 'S' represents a stimulus (or cue) and 'R' represents the response to this cue. The S–R bond is stored in the long-term memory. The connection of the S–R bond is strengthened by **reinforcement** — the process that causes behaviour to recur.

A practical example is a ball high in the air acting as a stimulus for a tennis player. The response to the stimulus is to hit the ball. If successful, the response connects with the stimulus and a learning bond is formed. If the response is ineffective, the S–R bond is weakened. (This is trial-and-error learning.)

Reinforcement can be given in two ways:
- **Positive reinforcement** involves the presentation of the stimulus of approval or a 'satisfier'. This could be in the form of verbal praise or a tangible reward. The aim is to encourage the correct action in the future.
- **Negative reinforcement** involves the withdrawal of praise offered for the correct response, or the use of punishment (e.g. extra training) for an incorrect response.

Thorndike's laws
Although learning can take place in various ways, the psychologist Thorndike believed that the most effective way to learn is to form and strengthen a learning bond through the application of reinforcement. Thorndike put forward three laws relating to the application of reinforcement.
- **Law of effect** — positive reinforcement increases the chance of behaviour reoccurring. (A coach should try to praise or reward performers when they are successful.)
- **Law of exercise** — the more often a response is reinforced, the stronger the learning bond will become.
- **Law of readiness** — learning by connecting can only take place when the nervous system has reached an appropriate stage of maturation.

Operant conditioning
Operant conditioning is a major connectionist theory put forward by the psychologist Skinner (1974). It is mainly concerned with responses rather than with stimuli.

There are a number of key points about operant conditioning that you need to know and be able to apply to a sports coaching situation. These include:
- manipulating or structuring a situation to bring about a desired response
- learning by trial and error

- reinforcing of the response (e.g. positive comments)
- changing the response, the process of which is termed 'behaviour shaping'

Cognitive learning theory

Cognitive theories emphasise the individual's thought processes as opposed to the influence of a stimulus and a response.

Key points

- **Gestalt theory** is the major cognitive theory.
- Cognitive psychologists Wertheimer and Köhler believed that learning is most effective through problem solving and that insight is a means of learning.
- This approach is in direct contrast to the connectionist belief.
- A cognitive process is a thinking process.
- Generally, learning a skill takes place quite slowly in the early stages and then quite rapidly later.

According to cognitive theory, for learning to occur, five factors must be in place:

- **Perception** — interpretation or understanding of the whole task. For example, difficulty encountered in the execution of a vault may be eased if the gymnast is made aware of, and understands, the mechanics of the movement.
- **Previous experience** — related experience can help to establish insight into how a new task is to be performed. For example, the experience of throwing a ball relates to learning to serve in tennis. This is transfer of learning.
- **Current knowledge** — the learner needs an insight into what is required — for example, the strategies required to defeat a full court press in basketball.
- **Motivation** — the learner must be motivated to solve the problem.
- **Self-esteem** — learning can be accomplished only if the novice has positive self-perception.

Applying cognitive theory therefore involves a period of purposeful experimentation in which the learner uses experience, knowledge and perception to solve the whole problem.

In practical terms, this means that skills are best learned by conditioning or by adapting games, rather than by perfecting techniques in isolation. For example, a Gestaltist would argue that short tennis is a better introduction to tennis than teaching separate shots. Mechanical guidance can be used to simplify the whole skill. For example, a tumbling harness can help the learning of a somersault in trampolining or a buoyancy aid can help the novice swimmer to experience the 'feeling of tone' of the whole stroke.

According to Gestalt theory, the solution to the whole problem may emerge suddenly. This is called the **eureka phenomenon.**

Observational learning

The psychologist Bandura believed that learning was most effectively achieved by imitating or copying others.

The theory of observational learning involves watching a demonstration and replicating the model. The learner must display four factors before learning can be achieved through observation. These factors are summarised in the table below.

Factor	Learner	Coach
Attention	Must focus concentration on the model	Can highlight the key areas of the skill
Retention	Must remember the image	Should give a clear, correct image so it can be remembered
Motor reproduction	Must have the necessary ability and skill to replicate the demonstration	Should make sure the performer is physically capable of performing the skill
Motivation	Must have the drive to learn	Can reward or praise the performer to create the drive to learn

Coaches can use Bandura's model of observational learning to help a performer to progress.

Phases of movement skill learning

The psychologists Fitts and Posner put forward the idea of three learning phases or stages, which relate directly to the acquisition of motor skills.

Learning phases

The cognitive phase
This is the thinking stage. The key points are as follows:
- The learner engages in mental rehearsal and benefits from observing a demonstration.
- By the end of this phase, the learner attempts to perform the skill.
- Feedback needs to be both extrinsic and positive, to highlight errors in performance.

The associative phase
This is the practice stage in which the learner participates physically. The key points are as follows:
- The response is inefficient and often incorrect.
- The learner requires great concentration during performance.
- Mental rehearsal can help learning and develop fluency.
- Demonstration remains important and reinforcement should be positive.
- Control of the skill is largely through external feedback (KR).
- The learner begins to use intrinsic or kinaesthetic feedback (KP) to control the skill.

The autonomous phase
This is the expert stage, at which the skill can be executed automatically. The key points are as follows:

- The movement has been 'grooved' or over-learned.
- The correct response can now be associated with the correct 'feeling tone'.
- Attention can be given to peripheral environmental cues.
- Demonstration and mental rehearsal remain important.
- The expert uses intrinsic feedback for self-correction (KP).
- Negative extrinsic feedback from the coach assists fault correction and helps in fine tuning.

Methods of guidance

There are four types of guidance that can be used to help the learning process:

- **Visual guidance** can be in the form of a precise demonstration showing the action or displaying changes. Chalking the ground during bowling practice in cricket to give the learner a target is an example. Visual guidance is best used at the cognitive stage of learning, as it registers an image for a longer time than other methods of guidance and can be easily absorbed by the learner.
- **Verbal guidance** involves telling the learner what to do. It is of more benefit for the learning of open skills that require decision-making and perceptual judgements. Verbal guidance is best used at the autonomous stage of learning and is less relevant to beginners.
- **Manual guidance** involves the coach holding and physically 'shaping' the body to give the learner an idea of how the skill should feel (e.g. learning a tennis serve).
- **Mechanical guidance** makes use of an object or piece of apparatus to shape the skill (e.g. a gymnastic harness).

Note that manual and mechanical guidance have some drawbacks associated with them. For example, they are not given in the 'real game' situation, so their overuse could result in negative transfer. There is also the risk that the learner becomes reliant on the type of guidance. They are of limited use in large group situations and with fast, complex movements. However, they can be used to give support or confidence in potentially dangerous situations.

Transfer of learning

Transfer is the process of one skill influencing the learning and performance of a separate skill. This is an important topic — practically all learning is based on some form of transfer.

You need to know about five types of transfer and to be able to apply them to practical examples:

- **Positive transfer** occurs when one skill helps the learning and performance of another — for example, two skills that have similar forms, such as a tennis serve and an overarm volleyball serve.
- **Negative transfer** is evident when one skill impairs the learning and performance of another. For example, the wrist actions in tennis and squash are completely

different. A fixed wrist in tennis can have negative effects in squash, which requires a flexible wrist.

- **Proactive transfer** takes place when a previously learned skill influences the learning and performance of later skills, either positively or negatively. For example, learning to throw overarm as a child will later help the racquet arm action when learning to serve in tennis.
- **Retroactive transfer** occurs when new skills influence the learning and performance of old skills, either positively or negatively. For example, learning a tennis serve as a student could influence the throwing skills that were acquired in childhood.
- **Bilateral transfer** is the transfer of learning from limb to limb. An example would be a player with a dominant right foot learning to kick with the left.

To try to ensure that positive transfer takes place when teaching a sports skill, a coach can:

- ensure the two skills involved are sufficiently alike for transfer to occur
- practise or give experience of the original task
- provide realistic practice or game scenarios
- give a similar stimulus/response/movement pattern
- make the performer aware of the potential for transfer
- explain the mechanical principles or key elements behind the skill and ensure that the learner is involved in skill analysis

It is important that you are aware of the link between schema theory and transfer of learning. Schema is an accumulation of knowledge and motor programmes that can be adapted and transferred to help a response to a new situation.

Motivation and arousal

Motivation is the psychological wish, desire or drive to succeed and perform well in sport. **Arousal** is the degree of excitement or activation that prepares the person for performance.

Learning and performance of motor skills cannot take place without a degree of motivation.

Intrinsic motivation

Intrinsic motivation is inner drive and self-satisfaction (e.g. mastery for its own sake).

Advantages
- Longer lasting than extrinsic motivation
- Good for youngsters to place more emphasis on fun and enjoyment (etc.) than on trophies or praise

Disadvantages
- Less relevant in professional sport

- Difficult for some people to generate enough intrinsic motivation to continue participating in an activity

Extrinsic motivation

Extrinsic motivation is when motivation comes from an outside source such as praise from a coach or the possibility of an award or trophy. Extrinsic reward is a valuable motivator for a beginner, but will eventually undermine intrinsic motivation.

Advantages
- Material rewards increase the probability of a particular behaviour occurring again
- Motivates individuals to continue involvement

Disadvantages
- Overuse of extrinsic motivation can lead to a decrease in intrinsic motivation
- Rewards can transform what was regarded as a 'fun' activity into a chore

Motivation has two components:
- **Intensity of behaviour** is the degree of physical and emotional energy displayed by the individual. This is known as **arousal**.
- **Direction of behaviour** is the way arousal is used to reach a goal or target.

Drive theory

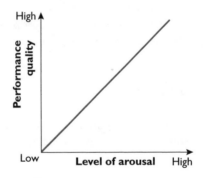

- Drive theory proposes that as arousal increases, there is a proportional increase in the quality of performance.
- The quality of performance depends upon how well the skill has been learned.
- Actions that have been learned are called dominant responses.
- Dominant responses are the actions that are most likely to occur as arousal increases.

Implications for teaching and learning
- In the associative phase of learning, the dominant response is likely to be incorrect. Therefore, the novice learns best when in a condition of low arousal.
- In the autonomous phase of learning, an expert performs better in an environment that stimulates high arousal.

The inverted-U theory

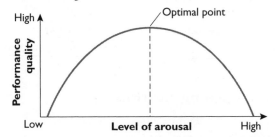

The inverted-U theory predicts that as arousal increases, the quality of performance and the capacity to concentrate improve and are at their best at the optimum point. The optimum point is also called the 'threshold of arousal'. It occurs midway along the arousal axis. After the optimal point, if arousal continues to increase, the capacity to perform and concentrate will decline.

Implications of under-arousal for teaching and learning
- The attention field (the environment of which we are aware) widens excessively.
- The learner is not able to selectively attend to the most relevant cues.
- An information overload will result.

Implications of over-arousal for teaching and learning
The attention field narrows excessively, causing relevant cues to be missed. In this condition, the learner may experience high anxiety or panic. The technical term for this condition is **hypervigilance**.

Optimal arousal
At optimal arousal:
- the attention field adjusts to the ideal width
- the learner is able to selectively attend to the relevant environmental cues and process information effectively (**cue utilisation**)
- concentration is at a maximum

Drive reduction theory

The initial drive to learn the skill is strong, but once the skill is learned, drive is reduced. As a result, the performance quality of the skill will decline.

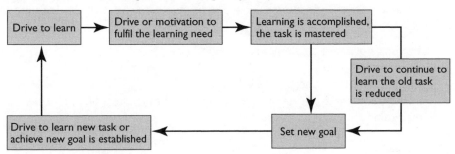

Implications for teaching and learning
- The drive to learn must be maintained.
- To replenish the drive, new targets should be introduced.
- Drive reduction could occur because of boredom through repetition.
- Practices should vary.

Strategies to increase motivation

Strategies to increase the motivation to learn include:
- positively reinforcing the learner's performance
- providing extrinsic rewards
- ensuring that learning targets are challenging and realistic
- appropriately changing the practice or drill to attain a specific goal (variability of practice)
- making use of role models
- presenting the skill as a worthwhile element to learn
- making the learner aware of how progressions can be made
- ensuring that practices are fun.

Practice conditions

Massed practice

Massed practice is a practice session with no breaks. It is used when the task is simple and discrete, and when motivation and ability of the group are high.

The advantages of massed practice are that:
- more physical work is possible in a single session
- it allows the learner to experience the flow of the whole skill
- it is good for the development of kinaesthesis

Distributed practice

Distributed practice includes breaks, so the session is divided into short periods. It is used when the task is complex and continuous, and the ability of the group is low. Distributed practice is more effective than massed practice in the learning of motor skills.

The advantages of distributed practice are that:
- it allows periods of rest
- feedback and performance analysis can be given
- it enables learners to engage in **mental rehearsal** to create a picture of the skill in their minds

What the examiner will expect you to be able to do

- You need to be able to describe the key characteristics of each of the three phases of learning. It is also important that you are able to differentiate between the cognitive phase of learning and the cognitive theory of learning, so that in the examination you do not misinterpret a question and give an answer that earns no marks.
- You should know the difference between positive and negative reinforcement — positive reinforcement involves a pleasant stimulus such as praise for a correct response; negative reinforcement means the withdrawal of approval when a desired response prevails.
- It is important that you learn Thorndike's laws so that you are able to show how to make the S–R bond stronger. You will be expected to know the difference between positive and negative transfer and to be able to use appropriate examples to illustrate your understanding.
- Questions on motivation usually focus on either an explanation of the difference between extrinsic and intrinsic motivation or on the methods that could be used to motivate a sports performer. It is important that you show clear knowledge of these methods and that you can use examples from sport to illustrate them.

Questions
&
Answers

This section of the guide contains questions that are similar in style to those you can expect to see in Unit Test 1. The questions cover the four areas of physiological factors and the four areas of psychological factors covered by the **Module 1: Physiological and Psychological Factors which Improve Performance**.

Each question is followed by an average or poor response (Candidate A) and an A-grade response (Candidate B).

You should try to answer these questions yourself, so that you can compare your answers with the candidates' responses. In this way, you should be able to identify your strengths and weaknesses in both subject knowledge and exam technique.

Examiner's comments

All candidate responses are followed by examiner's comments. These are preceded by the icon 🄴 and indicate where credit is due. In the weaker answers they also point out areas for improvement, specific problems and common errors, such as vagueness, irrelevance and misinterpretation of the question.

Question 1

Movement

(a) The preparation phase for the jump shown in the diagram below involves a downward movement.

Complete the table below to show the types of joint and joint action involved, the main agonist and the type of contraction that occurs during this downward phase.

(9 marks)

	Type of joint	Joint action	Agonist	Type of contraction
Hip		Flexion		
Knee				Eccentric
Ankle	Hinge			

(b)

With reference to the knee-joint of the kicking leg of the footballer:

(i) Name the articulating bones. (2 marks)

(ii) At the moment leading up to impact, what joint action is taking place at the knee-joint and what is the name of the agonist causing this action? (2 marks)

Total: 13 marks

Candidates' answers to Question 1

Candidate A

(a)

	Type of joint	Joint action	Agonist	Type of contraction
Hip	Ball and socket ✓	Flexion	Hamstrings ✓	Isotonic ✓
Knee	Hinge ✓	Flexion ✓	Quads	Eccentric
Ankle	Hinge	Flexion	Gastrocnemius ✓	Isotonic

> *e* This response lacks sufficient detail. You must be specific. The movement in the ankle joint is *dorsiflexion* — flexion alone will not score the mark. Abbreviating muscle names will also prevent a mark being awarded — for example, 'quads' is not an acceptable answer, whereas 'quadriceps' is. Similarly, you need to be specific about the type of muscle contraction. By using 'isotonic' twice, Candidate A is limited to 1 mark. To gain both the available marks for contraction, the candidate should have given the *type* of isotonic contraction, i.e. eccentric. Candidate A scores 6 of the 9 marks available.

Candidate B

(a)

	Type of joint	Joint action	Agonist	Type of contraction
Hip	Ball and socket ✓	Flexion	Hamstrings ✓	Eccentric ✓
Knee	Hinge ✓	Flexion ✓	Quadriceps ✓	Eccentric
Ankle	Hinge	Dorsiflexion ✓	Gastrocnemius ✓	Eccentric ✓

> *e* There is 1 mark available for each correct answer in the table. The candidate has correctly identified the types of joint, the joint action, the muscles involved and the types of contraction and scores all 9 marks.

Candidate A

(b) Femur ✓ and fibula. The movement is extension ✓ and the agonists are the hamstrings.

> *e* One common mistake candidates make is to name the fibula as one of the articulating bones of the knee joint. This bone actually stops before it reaches the knee. Candidates also often confuse the movement produced by the hamstrings and the quadriceps. This is an easy mark lost. With more revision, Candidate A would have remembered that the hamstrings flex the knee and the quadriceps extend the knee. Candidate A scores 2 marks.

Candidate B

(b) Femur ✓ and tibia ✓. The joint action is extension ✓ and the agonist is the quadriceps ✓.

☑ This is a top-level answer. All the bones, movement and muscles are correctly identified. Thorough revision of the sporting actions required by the specification will ensure success. Candidate B scores all 4 marks.

☑ **Overall, Candidate A scores 8 out of 13 marks; Candidate B scores 13.**

uestion **2**

Levers

Name the lever system that operates at the elbow during flexion. Sketch and label a diagram to show this type of lever. (3 marks)

Total: 3 marks

■ ■ ■

Candidates' answers to Question 2

Candidate A

This is a third-order lever ✓.

e The candidate clearly knows the correct answer but has omitted to label the fulcrum. This means that a mark is lost. Make sure you check all your answers, so that you do not lose easy marks. Candidate A scores 2 marks.

Candidate B

This is a third-order lever ✓.

e The type of lever is correctly identified and the diagram is fully labelled. Candidate B scores 3 marks.

e **Candidate A scores 2 out of 3 marks; Candidate B scores 3.**

Question 3

Fitness

(a) **Identify two important fitness components that are required by a sprint swimmer. Give an example of how one of these components is used within a race.** (3 marks)

(b) **A timed 30 m sprint can be used as a test for power. Discuss whether this test is valid *and* reliable for high jumpers.** (4 marks)

Total: 7 marks

■ ■ ■

Candidates' answers to Question 3

Candidate A

(a) Speed ✓ and power ✓ are two fitness components required by a sprint swimmer.

> ✐ Having correctly identified two fitness components required by a sprint swimmer, Candidate A then forgets to say how one of these components is used during a race. Always read the question carefully and check your answer. Looking at the marks available for a question should indicate the number of points required. Candidate A scores 2 marks.

Candidate B

(a) Speed ✓ and reaction time ✓ are required by a sprint swimmer. Reaction time is needed to get a fast start off the starting blocks ✓.

> ✐ This candidate names two relevant fitness components required by a sprint swimmer and then goes on to say when one of these is important in a race. It is important that you choose the fitness components that are most relevant to the sporting activity asked. Candidate B scores all 3 marks.

Candidate A

(b) A high jumper needs to jump up into the air. The 30 m sprint test does not test for this, so it is not valid ✓. However, the high jumper does need speed and strength and these are tested by the 30 m sprint ✓, so it is reliable.

> ✐ Here, Candidate A has given reasons why the 30 m sprint test can be considered to be both valid and invalid. However, no explanation has been given of reliability, despite the use of the term in the second part of the answer. You should make sure that you are clear about the differences between validity and reliability. Candidate A scores 2 marks.

Candidate B

(b) A valid test should measure exactly what it sets out to do. The 30 m sprint involves strength and speed, which are valid for a high jumper ✓. However, it is not sport specific because it does not reflect the high-jumping action ✓. Reliability concerns

the accuracy of the test. This test is repeatable ✓, but the performer must be motivated to complete it ✓.

e This is a top-level answer. The candidate clarifies validity and reliability, which makes it easier to explain the relevance of the test to the high jumper. There are 4 marks available and four correct points made, so Candidate B scores full marks.

e **Overall, Candidate A scores 4 out of 7 marks; Candidate B scores 7.**

Question 4

Respiration

(a) The breathing characteristics of games players alter during performance. The table below shows the percentages of oxygen and carbon dioxide breathed out during exercise compared with at rest.

Gas	Inhaled air	Exhaled air (quiet breathing)	Exhaled air (exercise)
Oxygen/%	21	17	15
Carbon dioxide/%	0.04	4	6

Use the information in the table to describe the effects of exercise on gas exchange in the lungs. Suggest why these changes occur. (3 marks)

The table below shows how measures concerned with breathing change during the performance of an exercise programme.

Measure	Rest	Exercise
Breathing rate/breaths min^{-1}	20	25
Tidal volume/cm^3	500	2000
Vital capacity/cm^3	5000	5000

(b) Explain the causes of the increase in breathing rate experienced during exercise. (4 marks)

(c) Calculate the minute volume at rest. (2 marks)

Total: 9 marks

■ ■ ■

Candidates' answers to Question 4

Candidate A

(a) From the table, there is more oxygen consumed. This is because it is needed for energy ✓.

> 🄔 This question requires the candidates to look at the whole table. Therefore, an answer that mentions just one gas will automatically lose 1 mark. The candidate should also have referred to carbon dioxide. In this response, the fact that Candidate A has only mentioned oxygen affects the second part of the answer too, and a second mark is lost. Candidate A scores 1 mark only.

Candidate B

(a) From the table, it can be seen that during exercise there is more oxygen taken in and more carbon dioxide breathed out ✓. The oxygen is needed for energy ✓ and the carbon dioxide is a waste product ✓.

e This response is detailed and covers all parts of the question. When a table is presented in a question, always make sure that you refer to it comprehensively. Candidate B scores all 3 marks.

Candidate A

(b) During exercise, there is an increase in the production of carbon dioxide ✓. As a result, impulses are sent to the medulla ✓, which sends impulses to the lungs to increase breathing rate.

e With a little more detail, this answer could have gained full marks. Candidate A identifies an increase in carbon dioxide but does not say that this is detected by chemoreceptors. Saying that an impulse goes to the lungs is almost correct. However, you are required to know exactly where the impulses are sent, i.e. to the respiratory muscles. Always give as much detail as possible! Candidate A scores 2 marks.

Candidate B

(b) There is an increase in the production of carbon dioxide ✓ and, therefore, blood acidity ✓. This is detected by chemoreceptors ✓. Impulses are sent to the respiratory centre in the medulla, ✓ which in turn sends impulses to the diaphragm and external intercostals ✓.

e Candidate B makes five correct points, one more than the number of marks allocated. Generally, with questions that do not specify a particular number, it is good exam technique to look at the mark allocation and make more points than there are marks available, in an attempt to ensure the possibility of a maximum mark. However, if a question specifies a number (e.g. 'Give two….') only the first two answers will be marked. Candidate B scores all 4 marks.

Candidate A

(c) $10\,dm^3$

e Candidate A gives the correct response of 10 dm³, but fails to gain the mark because 'per minute' is not specified. Attention to detail is important. The method of calculating minute ventilation is not given, so the second mark is lost. Candidate A fails to score.

Candidate B

(c) minute ventilation = breathing rate × tidal volume ✓
$$= 20 \times 500 = 10\,000\,cm^3 \text{ or } 10\,dm^3 ✓$$

e The calculation is clearly shown and the answer has the correct units. Always take a calculator into the exam, in case you are required to work out, for example, a lung volume or cardiac output. Candidate B scores both marks.

e **Overall, Candidate A scores 3 out of 9 marks; Candidate B scores 9.**

The cardiovascular system

(a) Heart rate and stroke volume both increase during exercise. What causes an increase in stroke volume? (2 marks)

(b) The heart rate increases before and during exercise and then decreases after exercise. Explain how these changes in heart rate occur. (4 marks)

(c) During exercise, the distribution of cardiac output to different parts of the body alters. This is summarised in the table below.

	Rate of blood flow/cm³ min⁻¹	
Body part	**At rest**	**During exercise**
Muscle	1 000	16 000
Heart muscle	300	1 200
Gut and liver	3 000	1 400
Brain	750	750
Other organs (not lungs)	1 550	1 550

State *three* reasons for an increase in cardiac output during exercise. (3 marks)

Total: 9 marks

■ ■ ■

Candidates' answers to Question 5

Candidate A

(a) An increase in stroke volume is caused by an increase in venous return ✓, which means more blood can be pumped out of the heart.

> 🖉 Only 1 mark can be awarded because the mark scheme classes the points as similar, i.e. one is the result of the other. Had the candidate made more points than the number of marks allocated, then both marks might have been gained.

Candidate B

(a) An increase in stroke volume is caused by an increase in the strength of contraction of the heart ✓. This means that more blood can be ejected by the heart ✓.

> 🖉 This answer gives two correct responses and scores both marks. The candidate could have said that an increase in stroke volume is also caused by adrenaline and by nervous control. It has also been correctly indicated that it is an increase in the strength of contraction that has caused more blood to be pumped out of the heart.

Candidate A

(b) Adrenaline causes an increase in heart rate before exercise ✓. During exercise, receptors detect changes, such as an increase in carbon dioxide ✓. They send impulses to the brain, which increase heart rate.

e Candidate A does not specify chemoreceptors and loses a mark. 'Brain' is too vague to score. The candidate should have mentioned the cardiac centre as well as the decrease in heart rate. Similarly, the SA node should have been cited, rather than simply 'heart.' There is a lack of detail in this mediocre answer. Candidate A scores 2 marks.

Candidate B

(b) An increase in heart rate prior to exercise is due to adrenaline ✓. During exercise, there is an increase in carbon dioxide ✓ and, therefore, an increase in acidity ✓. This is detected by chemoreceptors ✓ and an impulse is sent to the cardiac centre ✓. This, in turn, sends an impulse to the SA node to increase heart rate ✓. After exercise, the parasympathetic nervous system decreases heart rate ✓.

e This is a comprehensive answer. Candidate B has covered as many points as possible to try to gain the maximum mark. This is good exam technique. The candidate is aware that the nature of the question allows this approach to be taken. Candidate B scores all 4 marks.

Candidate A

(c) A rise in cardiac output occurs because of more blood flow, an increase in stroke volume ✓ and extra venous return. A rise in heart rate increase can also increase cardiac output.

e The question asks for three reasons. This means that in most cases, examiners will only mark the first three answers given. In this response, there are four reasons given. The fourth is correct but does not gain the mark. Always check, when a question specifies a particular number of answers, that you list *only* that number. Candidate A scores 1 mark only.

Candidate B

(c) An increase in cardiac output occurs during exercise because of:
- an increase in heart rate ✓
- an increase in stroke volume ✓
- an increase in the strength of contraction ✓

e This answer gives three correct responses, exactly as the question asks. Other correct responses are: a faster rate of firing of the SA node; increased diastolic filling; the release of adrenaline; a rise in carbon dioxide levels (lower pH) stimulating the chemoreceptors and an increase in sympathetic nervous system impulses. Candidate B scores all 3 marks.

e **Overall, Candidate A scores 4 out of 9 marks; Candidate B scores 9.**

Effects of training

Cardiorespiratory-endurance training causes changes to the structure and functioning of the body, which help to improve performance. Describe these changes in terms of both the heart *and* the lungs.

(4 marks)

Total: 4 marks

■ ■ ■

Candidates' answers to Question 6

Candidate A

The heart becomes much stronger ✓, so can pump out more blood. Lung volumes increase and there is increased lung efficiency ✓.

e The amount of blood the left ventricle can pump out per beat is called the stroke volume. Make sure that you use correct terminology — 'pumping out more blood' is too vague to score a mark. Lung volumes *and* capacities do increase as a result of training, but you need to say which, i.e. inspiratory reserve volume, expiratory reserve volume and, therefore, vital capacity. Candidate A scores 2 marks.

Candidate B

There is hypertrophy of the heart ✓. This allows an increase in stroke volume ✓ because more blood enters the left ventricle ✓. Bradycardia also occurs ✓. Lung volumes change very little with training but there is increased lung efficiency ✓.

e This response has lots of detail and makes more points than the number of marks allocated. This is good exam technique as it ensures the possibility of gaining full marks. Other correct responses include: a rise in maximum cardiac output; extra capillarisation and an increase in the force of contraction. In the lungs, there is greater ability to extract more oxygen. Candidate B scores all 4 marks.

e **Candidate A scores 2 out of 4 marks; Candidate B scores 4.**

Question 7

Stages of a sprint

The diagram below shows the various stages that occur prior to, during and at the end of a sprint.

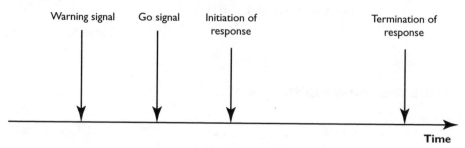

Redraw the diagram, and clearly label your drawing to identify *reaction time, movement time* and *response time*.

(3 marks)

Total: 3 marks

■ ■ ■

Candidates' answers to Question 7

Candidate A

Reaction time is the time it takes you to react. Movement time is the time it takes you to move. Response time is the time it takes you to respond.

e This answer shows that Candidate A has not read the question carefully. It requires a *clearly labelled drawing* showing a more detailed understanding of the concepts asked. The response is irrelevant and too vague to earn any marks.

Candidate B

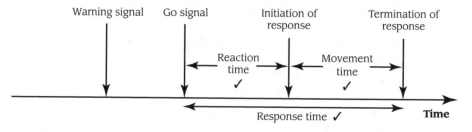

e This diagram illustrates clear understanding of reaction time (from 'go' to initiation of response), movement time (from initiation to termination of response) and response time (reaction time plus movement time). This answer contains correct information that is relevant to the question set, so Candidate B scores all 3 marks.

e **Candidate A fails to score; Candidate B scores all 3 marks.**

Hicks's law

The graph below illustrates Hicks's law.

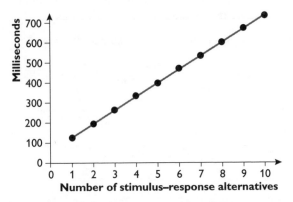

Use Hicks's law and the concept of the psychological refractory period to explain how an attacker in a team may gain an advantage over a defender.   (6 marks)

Total: 6 marks

■ ■ ■

Candidates' answers to Question 8

Candidate A

I think Hicks's law states that choice reaction time is affected by the number of choices that you have ✓. If you have more choices to make, it takes you longer to react. There is a linear relationship between choices and reaction time ✓. If you double the choices, you double the reaction time.

e The answer about Hick's law shows good understanding. There is some repetition of points made, but generally it is a good start. The problems with this answer are that it fails to link to the practical example asked for in the question and it ignores the reference to the psychological refractory period. Candidate A scores only 2 of the 6 marks available.

Candidate B

Hicks's law states that the more choices you have available, the longer it takes to react to them ✓. This relationship is linear ✓.

The psychological refractory period (PRP) explains why it takes longer to respond to a second stimulus ✓. It can be applied in games situations when you 'dummy' an opponent (e.g. in rugby when you fake a pass but carry on running with the ball) ✓. Your opponent responds to your first signal (the fake pass), before being able to respond to the second signal ✓, which means that you can move off past your opponent with the ball ✓.

question

e This is an excellent response, which is relevant to the question set and scores all 6 marks. Hicks's law and the PRP are both explained and linked to a practical games example. If more marks had been available, reference could have been made to the single-channel hypothesis linked to the PRP (i.e. the need to respond to the first signal received before the second signal can be dealt with).

e **Candidate A scores 2 out of 6 marks; Candidate B scores 6.**

Question 9

Feedback

(a) For a *novice* hockey player, 'effective feedback' is essential for progress.
What are the characteristics of 'effective feedback'? (3 marks)

(b) Explain how feedback differs as performers progress through the *associative*
and *autonomous* phases of learning. (4 marks)

Total: 7 marks

■ ■ ■

Candidates' answers to Question 9

Candidate A

(a) A hockey player needs lots of feedback from a coach in order to improve. This can be given while playing a game of hockey. Different methods might be used to give feedback, such as visual and verbal ✓.

> *e* The first two sentences are irrelevant to the novice or beginner. This illustrates a common fault — the candidate has failed to answer the question set. This could be avoided by reading the question, then re-reading it and highlighting key words. The final sentence is worthy of a mark as it makes a point that is relevant to the novice performer. Candidate A scores just 1 mark.

Candidate B

(a) Effective feedback for a novice hockey player would be:
- simple and relevant to the player ✓
- clear and accurate to help the novice player focus on what is important ✓
- immediate — as soon as the action is over ✓
- relevant to the individual ✓
- provided using different methods, such as verbal and visual feedback ✓

> *e* Candidate B scores the full 3 marks with the first three points. This is an excellent answer. It is succinct and relevant to the question set. More points are made than the marks allocated to try to ensure that the maximum mark is earned. This is good exam practice.

Candidate A

(b) As performers reach the associative phase of learning, they begin to be able to monitor their own feedback ✓. Feedback given by a coach will be a little more critical than that given at the cognitive stage ✓. At the associative stage, there will be more use of extrinsic, rather than intrinsic, feedback ✓.

> *e* This is an excellent answer to one part of the question, with three correct, relevant points. However, there are only 2 marks available for the associative phase and 2 marks for the autonomous phase. In questions with two or more parts to them, it is essential to give a balanced answer with relevant points about each part. By ignoring the autonomous phase of learning, 2 valuable marks are lost.

Candidate B

(b) At the associative stage of learning, performers are able to monitor their own feedback ✓. It may still be extrinsic to them ✓, but becomes a little more detailed and critical to help them improve.

As the autonomous stage is reached, performers become less reliant on knowledge of results ✓ and are able to detect their own errors with intrinsic feedback ✓.

🖉 Both parts of the question are answered, with correct points made in relation to the two phases of learning. Candidate B scores all 4 marks.

🖉 **Overall, Candidate A scores 3 out of 7 marks; Candidate B scores 7.**

Classification of skills

Performers in the women's heptathlon compete in seven different events:
100 m sprint, high jump, long jump, shot put, javelin, 800 m and 110 m hurdles.
Name, giving a *reason* for your choice, *one* heptathlon event that is mainly:

- **an open skill** (2 marks)
- **a continuous skill** (2 marks)
- **a serial skill** (2 marks)
- **a self-paced skill** (2 marks)

Total: 8 marks

■ ■ ■

Candidates' answers to Question 10

Candidate A

- An open skill — shot put
- A continuous skill — running 800 m ✓
- A serial skill — the high jump ✓
- A self-paced skill — throwing a javelin ✓

e Questions often have words in bold print and/or italics. Particular attention should be paid to such words because they are meant to help you focus on the key requirements of the question. Candidate A's response is a basic attempt at an answer, which earns 3 marks for events correctly linked to skill classifications. However, the candidate has not justified the choice of events with reasons. This limits the number of marks that can be gained.

Candidate B

- An open skill — the 800 m ✓. The external environment may change, which requires lots of instant decisions to be made ✓.
- A continuous skill — the 100 m ✓. Running has no distinct beginning and end ✓.
- A serial skill — the high jump ✓. It can be broken down and practised in parts ✓.
- A self-paced skill — the shot put ✓. It is started when the performer is ready to throw ✓.

e All parts of the question are answered correctly. A different event is given for each part of the question, thus ensuring that no marks are lost for repetition. If 100 m hurdles had been given as an example of both a continuous skill and a serial skill, then a mark could have been lost. Candidate B scores all 8 marks.

e **Candidate A scores 3 out of 8 marks; Candidate B scores 8.**

Theories of motor control

(a) **Explain, using an example, why closed-loop theory is not applicable to all skills.** (3 marks)

(b) **Schmidt's schema theory is based on** *four* **sources of information that are used to modify motor programmes. List the four sources of information.** (4 marks)

(c) **How can a coach organise practices to enable a schema to develop?** (3 marks)

Total: 10 marks

■ ■ ■

Candidates' answers to Question 11

Candidate A

(a) Some skills happen too quickly for feedback to be given ✓. They might be ballistic skills, ✓ which are very rapid.

> *e* The question asks for an example. Candidate A does not give an example but the answer shows clear understanding of closed-loop theory and its lack of relevance to all skills. Without an example, a mark is lost. In some cases, examiners might be instructed not to award any marks, so where examples are asked for, give them! Candidate A is lucky to score 2 marks.

Candidate B

(a) An example of a very rapid skill to which closed-loop theory is not relevant is a high serve in badminton ✓. It is over so quickly that there is no time for feedback ✓, so no corrections can be made while performing the skill ✓. Closed-loop theory is also not applicable to novel skills ✓.

> *e* Candidate B gives a relevant practical example at the beginning of the answer and makes three more correct points. Making more points than the mark allocation is good exam practice in trying to ensure scoring the maximum marks. In questions with relatively low marks, it is important to gain as many marks as possible, but not to waste time giving over-detailed responses. This might mean that you do not have enough time to answer properly more detailed questions with higher mark allocations. Candidate B scores all 3 marks.

Candidate A

(b) Sources of information could be a coach, a fellow performer, a teacher or the performer.

> *e* This answer is unfortunately far too vague and all the sources given are irrelevant. This indicates that Candidate A has either not understood or not revised Schmidt's schema theory. It is important to revise all the topics covered by the specification because any one of them can be examined. Vague, general answers will not lead to success at this level. Candidate A fails to score.

Candidate B

(b) The four sources of information used to modify motor programmes according to Schmidt's schema theory are:
- knowledge of initial conditions and/or skill requirements ✓
- knowledge of response demands — what is needed ✓
- KP — knowledge of performance ✓
- KR — knowledge of results ✓

e Four correct sources of information are given, which illustrates understanding of Schmidt's schema theory. When a specific number is asked for in the question, it is important to restrict yourself to that number. If, for example, four pieces of information are asked for, examiners may be told to mark the first four responses only. Candidate B scores the maximum 4 marks.

Candidate A

(c) Coaches can help a schema develop in a number of ways. For example, they can vary practice ✓ and avoid massed practice. By varying practice, performers can develop a schema for different sports.

e This answer shows poor exam technique by focusing on one particular point, and then repeating the information. To gain more marks, the response should contain a variety of relevant facts. Candidate A scores only 1 mark.

Candidate B

(c) To help a schema develop, practices should:
- use varied practice ✓
- give feedback ✓
- be linked to the game or activity ✓
- have parts that are transferable ✓
- have lots of information ✓

e Candidate B's answer shows excellent exam technique. The number of relevant points made exceeds the mark allocation. This is to ensure that there is a possibility of earning the maximum mark. No specific number of points is asked for, so giving a short introduction to a list of bullet points is an effective way of giving a number of responses in a relatively short space of time. Candidate B scores all 3 marks.

e **Overall, Candidate A scores 3 out of 10 marks; Candidate B scores 10.**

Memory

What are the characteristics of short-term memory? (6 marks)

Total: 6 marks

■ ■ ■

Candidates' answers to Question 12

Candidate A

Short-term memory has a very limited capacity of a few items (7±2) ✓. It only lasts a short time, from a second up to a minute or so ✓. After this time, information will be lost if it is not practised ✓.

ℓ This 6-mark question requires a much more detailed and varied response. All the points made are correct. However, a question with a relatively high mark allocation, should be given the time and exam-booklet space it deserves. Candidate A scores 3 marks.

Candidate B

Characteristics of short-term memory include the following:
- Information enters it from the short-term sensory store ✓.
- Only items receiving selective attention enter the short-term memory ✓.
- It is limited in capacity to 7±2 items ✓.
- Unless the information is put into practice, it will be lost ✓.
- Competing information interferes with information entering the short-term memory ✓.
- It is the working memory ✓.

ℓ This is an excellent list of characteristics of short-term memory. Factual recall is all that is needed in this type of 'what' question. One or two more points could have been made to try to ensure the maximum mark. This is just in case a point made is irrelevant or repeats a point that has already gained a mark. Candidate B scores all 6 marks.

ℓ **Candidate A scores 3 out of 6 marks; Candidate B scores 6.**

Question 13

Performance

(a) When observing the performance of a trampolinist, a coach might be trying to determine whether the performer is skilled or not. What are the characteristics of skilled performance? (3 marks)

(b) A coach 'reinforces' good performances during training by praising them. Why does this reinforcement work, rather than punishing poor performances? Explain your understanding of reinforcement and punishment in this situation. (5 marks)

(c) A swimming coach wants to improve the performance of the squad because the county championships are approaching. Using appropriate examples, what are the three main methods of guidance that the swimming coach can use to aid performance? (3 marks)

Total: 11 marks

■ ■ ■

Candidates' answers to Question 13

Candidate A

(a) A skilled trampolinist would perform in a correct way that would flow and look good ✓. The routine would be performed in a smooth manner and be aesthetically pleasing.

> *e* All the points made are correct and relevant, but they are too similar to gain more than 1 mark, which is awarded for the point made in relation to how a movement looks. To earn more marks, the candidate should have included a number of different points.

Candidate B

(a) Skilled performance is efficient ✓ with only a few mistakes ✓. It is smooth-flowing ✓ and can be adapted to situations as they arise ✓.

> *e* Four correct points are made in a succinct manner, ensuring that the maximum 3 marks are gained in a relatively short space of time. Unless the question asks for a specific number of points, it is always a good idea to try to make a few more relevant points than there are marks available.

Candidate A

(b) It is important to reinforce good performances in training by praise, such as telling the performers that they have done well. However, punishment is a negative, unpleasant experience for a sports performer ✓.

> *e* This answer is far too brief for a 5-mark question. It repeats the term 'reinforce' without rephrasing or expanding on it, which means that no marks can be awarded for this part of the answer. The candidate does attempt to answer both parts of the question, but the punishment part is far too brief. Candidate A scores only 1 mark.

Candidate B

(b) Reinforcement is something that gives satisfaction to the learner ✓ and leads to more motivation to do well ✓. Punishment is a negative experience (e.g. being shouted at and told off) ✓, which for many performers can lower their confidence ✓ and demotivate them. While reinforcement strengthens the S–R bond ✓, punishment weakens it.

> 🖉 Both parts of this question are answered in a relevant and relatively succinct manner. It is important not just to repeat terms as they appear in the question, but to reword and expand on them in order to meet the requirements of the task(s) set. Candidate B scores all 5 marks.

Candidate A

(c) Three good methods of guidance the coach can use are visual, verbal and manual.

> 🖉 The methods of guidance are all correct. However, they are not linked to swimming and practical examples have not been given. Therefore, Candidate A fails to score.

Candidate B

(c) The coach could use verbal guidance by using key words to help the swimmers improve (e.g. 'high elbow') ✓. Visual guidance could be used by, for example, showing videos or charts of how to do the stroke ✓. Manual guidance could be used by, for example, moving the performer's arms in an appropriate front-crawl action ✓.

> 🖉 Candidate B gives three correct forms of guidance, along with appropriate examples, which are specifically asked for in the question. In other words, this response answers the question set — an essential requirement for exam success! Candidate B scores all 3 marks.

> 🖉 **Overall, Candidate A scores 2 out of 11 marks; Candidate B scores 11.**